The *Un*American Dream

CARLOS HIDALGO

Copyright

The UnAmerican Dream By Carlos Hidalgo

Published by: Visum Publishing USA.
www.theunamericandream.com

ISBN-13: 978-1-937985-57-8
ISBN-10: 1-937985-57-1

Printed in the U.S.A.

Contents

Dedication

To Susanne . . . my best friend, my rock, my biggest supporter and encourager. You are the very definition of strength, grace and beauty. I love you!

What People Are Saying About
The UnAmerican Dream

"This book is a must read for anyone and everyone in leadership - no matter your industry. I not only enjoyed reading this book – I needed it. Carlos' story of his own life, his research of good science and the testimonies of other leaders all combine to sing over me a song I desperately needed to be reminded of: "You can rest."

— Brandi Lea; Executive Director
— Beauty for Ashes Uganda

"Most of these types of books are unrealistic and come from an ivory tower . . . this book comes from the heart."

— Craig Rosenberg; Co-Founder - Topo

"As someone who struggles with being obsessively driven at work while also being a loving father and devoted husband, The Unamerican Dream helped me discover that the person I am neglecting the most in all this hustle is the person I should take better care of – myself."

— Dave Lewis; Founder & CEO -
DemandGen International

"Human beings are wired for connection, but executives on the rise can easily lose sight of what is truly important.

As a therapist and couples' counselor, I see many clients whose identity is rooted in their career and wealth, yet they have lost connection with loved ones, community, and themselves. My husband and I discovered in our 30's that chasing the American Dream was costing us more than it was worth.

Recognizing the need to set work-life boundaries is a critical first step to creating a healthy, more fulfilling lifestyle for you and your family. Carlos offers thought-provoking questions to help you find clarity about what you value most.

The UnAmerican Dream comes at a time when our culture of consumerism is beginning to give way to the values of community, sustainability, and minimalism. I'm recommending this book to all my clients who are burned out, disconnected, and disenchanted with chasing the American Dream."

—Valerie Allen, MEd, LPCC, Mental Health Therapist and Couples Counselor, www.valallencounseling.com

Acknowledgements

A colleague of mine recently commented, "it has been a long road for you and this book." She was so right in so many ways. Writing this book has been a long road, but getting to the place where I was able to write it has been much longer and full of valuable lessons, hardships, peaks and valleys. There is no way I can thank all of those who have been a part of that journey, but I am very grateful for them all.

There are so many who have played a part in what you are holding in your hands and I am deeply grateful for their support, encouragement, listening ear and belief that what is in these pages is a story that needed to be told. I could write pages for all of those that played a role.

My deepest thanks and gratitude to the following:

James Carbary. You were the one who told me "Man, you have to write a book about this." You were the catalyst and I cannot thank you enough for your urging to write, review and provide your feedback.

Katie Martell, my friend and copy editor. Your positive outlook, vision, friendship and careful eye have been a true gift! Thank you for all that you have poured into Susanne and I and this book, it truly would not be what it is without you.

Brian Carroll, my dear friend and brother. Thank you for being willing to review early drafts, provide honest feedback, send articles you have found and be a sounding board. I value our conversations and our friendship.

There are so many others that I must also thank. Mom and Dad, thank you for your prayers and support throughout this journey. My in-laws, John and Marty, your support, guidance and love over the years are overwhelming and I cannot thank you enough as we would not be here if it were not for you. Michael and Beth, your grace, words of encouragement, challenges and friendship means more than you will ever know. John and Stacey, you two are amazing. Thank you for all your love and support. Mel Grusing, your wisdom and insights into life have been invaluable to me and have shaped me in incredible ways. I am deeply grateful. Tim Washer, your encouragement, friendship and prayers are treasured and started at the bottom of an escalator for which I will always be grateful. Andrew Davis, thank you for having the courage to tell me to "pull the ripcord." Jim Woodcock, thank you for walking with me through the hardest of times and sharing your heart and wisdom. Chris Arrendale, I am better for our friendship and continue to learn from you. Samantha Stone, thanks for letting me pick your brain and for the many recommendations you made throughout the process. Jon Gettings, your time, prayers and words of affirmation throughout this process have been a true gift for which I thank you! Randi Drinkwater, thank you for your friendship and for taking a risk on submitting me for the TEDx event. John Common, thanks for your friendship and listening to the talk track in my head about this book. Matt Vander Wiele, your words of advice, wisdom and brotherhood over the many years have impacted me deeply and I will forever cherish our relationship. Kristin Hege and the Convey team, you guys are awesome!

Thanks to all of those as well who allowed me to share their stories and our conversations.

Jonathan & Becca, Jeremy, Lauren and Luke; I love being your dad and thank you for all you have taught me in this journey.

And lastly but most importantly to my beloved Susanne, to whom this entire book is dedicated. Your belief in me, your love and support, your strength and your courage are overwhelming. You are my hero in every sense of the word and I could never express how deeply grateful I am for you and how much I love you. Your thumb prints are all over this book and my life.

Foreword

The one big thing I'm always looking out for in everything I do is authenticity. The best stories are truthful and the most valuable insights are bullsh*t free. This applies to the people I want to connect with too - grounded, honest people like Carlos Hidalgo.

That's why I'm humbled to write a foreword for his new book, *The UnAmerican Dream* – a story about losing focus and control, but reinventing something new on your own terms.

What is it that connects us as Americans? It's a belief in the power of community, helping others, shared values, and respect. But Carlos believes that along the way, we've distorted what the dream is, and decided it can be measured by your bank balance. We're defining each other by our professional aspirations and our ability to keep on hustling and never switching off.

But where does that leave you?

If you're building your business and growing your career in a way that alienates you from your own community, whether that's locally or in your own home, Carlos questions whether you're really living the American Dream after all. Are you living out your values? The pursuit of an ideal is natural, but stopping, checking yourself and taking stock of everything you're personally sacrificing along the way is a worthwhile conversation. After all, the top can be lonely when you don't have strong relationships around you or good wellbeing.

Carlos and I have trod a similar path and some of the parallel experiences shared from afar really drew me in to his story, shared in the pages ahead. We are both successful entrepreneurs who built up our own agencies, both becoming disillusioned with the hectic, 24/7 lifestyle that was alienating us from the core values and principles we live by. We both arrived at a crossroads that made us reassess every decision we'd made in our lives up until that point.

Most importantly, we both decided to make huge personal and professional shifts, leaping into the dark towards a better future. Our decisions were based on a desire to re-define our own success, instead of haplessly moving in a direction that not only felt unfulfilling but was also chipping away at our own sense of self.

I'm sure that anyone reading this foreword can think back to a time in your life where you've felt conflicted. You might have been successful in monetary terms as you climbed the corporate ladder or built your business, but at the end of every day, you may feel tired. Perhaps success isn't what you thought it would feel like.

This book is for anyone who's getting bogged down with feelings of dissatisfaction and unhappiness when every objective metric is constantly telling us we should be pleased and content to carry on. We should be obsessively accumulating material possessions, right?

The theme that darts throughout *The UnAmerican Dream* is pure, unadulterated honesty and it's so refreshing. Carlos opens himself up to you, the reader, and his thoughtful style is persuasive and compels us to choose a mindset that prioritizes contentment, instead of a dog-eat-dog fight to the top.

What I loved was the time and space Carlos gives his wife of 24 years, Susanne in the book – her perspective is invaluable and helps communicate the impact that "hustle culture" can have on someone's family and loved ones. We rarely hear about the experiences of the people who surround a successful person. Rarely do we hear their take on the loneliness, empty promises, disconnection, and sacrifices they, as partners, have to make too. Carlos doesn't shy away from inviting Susanne to explore her feelings – another testament to the book's commitment to truth.

Carlos empowers readers to manage their life in a healthier, less ego-driven way, which is only strengthened by his own personal experience and stories he's collected along the way. It's a highly engaging book that's perfect for navigating your way through a detached society.

Frankly, it's illuminating to read an entrepreneur grapple with philosophical questions and hard truths about work that are central to how we really want our society to look. Carlos gives valuable insight into how to establish boundaries and bring back the ethos of a healthy work-life balance when it seems more difficult than ever before to find.

**— Bryan Kramer; Best Selling Author, Keynote &
TED Speaker; Forbes Columnist**

Introduction

I absolutely knew it was time to quit when I hit rock bottom.

I finally made the choice early in the summer of 2016, as I had been wrestling for months with the decision to leave the marketing agency I co-founded eleven years prior. This is also when the idea for the *UnAmerican Dream* came to me.

Someone once told me the title made this sound like an "angry book." But, in the time since that summer, I've lived through a gauntlet of other emotions while processing many thoughts and decisions (and their inevitable consequences).

Sure, anger played a role. But fear, shame, regret, pride, humility, and finally, hope have all shaped the experience of making the hardest, but best professional decision of my life. Here's my story.

By all accounts, my gamble to leave a promising career as a software marketing executive in 2005 to co-found an agency was paying off. Our team was growing; we were acquiring brand-name clients and earning a great reputation in our industry. Additionally, my personal brand was growing; I was being recognized as a "thought leader;" I was making more money; I was earning industry accolades; I led our agency to two straight Inc. 5000 placements and published a book that was named an Amazon Top New Release.

It felt like living the dream of any entrepreneur. This is why we do what we do as business leaders, right? Isn't the goal to reap the lustrous rewards of tireless efforts, while spending countless hours obsessed with success?

Isn't this the American Dream?

It was only after some serious life choices and deep reflection that I realized how perverted this concept has become for so many.

Despite my dogged determination to pursue this "dream," and despite the pockets of success I did experience, I was not ever really happy. I was certainly not fulfilled, and I had grown restless. The more I pursued the hustle, the more time it asked of me, and the more I grew irritable and narcissistic. Ultimately, I had become a complete workaholic.

My relationships with my family and friends suffered, and the paradox became clear. The harder I worked, the more elusive the happiness that was supposed to accompany this dream became. The more I grasped at my entrepreneurial success to make me feel successful, the less I felt so.

What was going on? What *really* was this "dream" I was seeking? I had worked so hard and put everything else on the back burner so that I could grow a business, all so I could "make my mark." Even then, when I reached what seemed like a peak, all that was ahead of me was more climbing and grappling. I knew something had to change, and I knew I couldn't be the only one who felt this way.

What triggered this realization for me was a personal crisis which served as a wake-up call.

For a number of years my wife and kids had been asking for more time, letting me know that I was not as engaged as they needed and that my attention was continually diverted. I was never fully present.

For a few months at the agency, I did make changes, adjusting my schedule, reducing my travel and working hard to renew relationships I had neglected for far too long. However, I had to do more. I had to make some drastic changes.

One day, a fork in the road finally came, and a decision had to be made. Was I going to continue to pursue my business interests, chase "the dream," add to the growth, and risk losing my family? Or, was I going to get my priorities straight, realign my focus, make amends and change?

I finally made a life changing decision in October of 2016 to leave the agency I had put so much into in order to get my life back. I made the announcement about my leaving the company in the following LinkedIn post the following February:

> In his book, *No Mud, No Lotus,* author and Buddhist monk Thich Nhat Hanh says the following, "there is a kind of joy that comes from letting go." This is a very true statement and today I am letting go. I am letting go of ANNUITAS and moving onto my next chapter; one that is still being written and yet for me has tremendous clarity.
>
> The last eleven years have been the most rewarding of my professional career. What started as two guys hanging a shingle and declaring "open for business" has grown to a world-class team and one of the leading demand generation consultancies in the B2B marketing industry. I could not be more proud of the people of ANNUITAS and have had the

honor and privilege of leading this organization and working with some of the best and brightest minds in marketing and will always be thankful for that.

In a post I wrote on LinkedIn in April of 2016, I quoted Brené Brown, who talks about what we must cultivate for a wholehearted life. In my article I commented, "To truly cultivate, one must prioritize and be purposeful to cultivate what is deemed most important to them." And it is for this reason I am leaving ANNUITAS.

While over the last eleven years I have worked diligently for our customers and team members here at ANNUITAS, spent countless hours with clients, traveled more miles than I care to think about and been successful in building a business, it came at a cost and it was a cost that I should not have paid. It came at a cost to my family and that is a cost I am no longer willing to pay and it is with this in mind that I am moving on . . . to cultivate that which is most important to me. And while I will be staying in the industry and doing what I know, I am continually making and committed to a different list of priorities.

I am thankful for the opportunity I had over this last decade plus at ANNUITAS and see nothing but a bright future for them as they continue their success. However, I am more excited about the future that lies ahead for me, the decision I have made and the work I will be able to do going forward.

The response to this post was overwhelming. Many of the comments and personal notes included wishes of success and encouragement. However, what I did not expect was the wave of emails and phone calls I received from colleagues who, like me, were running their own businesses or leaping up the corporate ladder, yet were also questioning why. One asked, "How did you do it? I am completely miserable and I hardly see my family. I want to stop but I'm not sure how." Another vice-president who held a role in a Fortune 500 organization called, telling me that while he enjoyed his work, it was taking a toll on him relationally, physically and mentally. He also knew he could not continue, but did not know the steps to take.

Their heartfelt admissions were not only affirmation of my personal decision, but also taught me that I was not the only one whose idea of the American Dream was not all I hoped it would be.

This is in no way an angry book, but an honest book of my experience. My hope is that this book is one that invites you to think of work, achievement and professional success on your own terms. This book is for those like me, many of whom I have spoken to in the last few years, who are chasing something in the hopes that it will produce an outcome of happiness, but realizing that no matter how hard they chase, they, like me, end up with nothing of substance and risk losing what they truly hold most dear.

This book is for entrepreneurs, corporate executives or anyone on the fast track to corporate success who may be asking the question, "what is this all for?"

This book is for those who are living on a continual treadmill in the pursuit of the American Dream, and just want permission to step off from it.

This book is for those who want to build their own business or achieve success in a corporate structure, but who perhaps seek an honest perspective on entrepreneurship. It is for those who want to re-define what success looks like on their terms.

This book is also for my family. As I share my story, it is undoubtedly intertwined with theirs. By sharing our experience, my hopes are to challenge the culture we live in that says more is better, money equals success and happiness is realized by the number of zeros on your paycheck and the title you hold.

This book is for everyone who is chasing or has chased the American Dream only to find out along the way that it seems rather UnAmerican, unfulfilling, and not at all what we thought it would be. It's for those who are waking up to the reality that the American Dream has become a warped, dangerous reality in modern culture.

I am in no way writing to condemn those who have chosen the relentless path of business ownership or achieving rank within a corporation. Who am I to say that you have chosen the wrong journey? However, for those with an inkling that there could be something better, this book is for you.

My life changes are a continual work in progress and one of those is this book. To those who are reading, I thank you for taking the time to do so and hope in some small way this book will be helpful as you pursue your dream.

One more note to the reader:

In writing this book, I had a friend recommend that at the end of each chapter I put a few questions so readers could reflect. I hope they will be helpful along your journey.

I also hope you will take the time to ponder these questions, as many of them are ones that I had to ask myself. I found that the answers were not always easy to come by. At times I would go back and change my answers. I spent time processing my thoughts and answers with my wife and friends and these are still questions I ask as a means to ensure I am continually on a path to true success. I trust they are helpful to you wherever you may be on this journey.

Additionally, throughout this book I tell stories of those I have encountered along the way. In some of these stories I have used different names.

CHAPTER 1

Life, Liberty and the Pursuit of Happiness?

"It's a helluva start, being able to recognize what makes you happy." —*Lucille Ball*

I am sitting in a coffee shop in downtown Colorado Springs, CO as I write this chapter, (I find that coffee shops are often the best place to write). Over my left shoulder is a blackboard, the kind that those in my generation and before will remember from grade school.

The chalkboard invites patrons to write whatever they choose and it is full of messages, song lyrics, political statements, words of encouragement and words of lament. It is a blackboard full of anonymous outpouring from those who had something to say.

Out of all of the hundreds of messages that are written on the board, there is one that has caught my eye today. In small, diagonal letters written in yellow chalk is the single phrase: "Feel Alive."

I'm reminded of the quote from American professor of literature Joseph Campbell, who said "I don't believe people are looking for the meaning of life as much as they are looking for the experience of being alive."

I couldn't agree more. It is an extraordinary and beautiful experience to truly feel alive, to come into tune with your true self. True happiness is truly feeling alive!

Unfortunately, I spent a good number of years, dare I say decades, trying to feel alive based on what I did professionally, completely out of harmony with who I am. I thought I could discover that feeling in my professional achievements, corporate rank and business accolades.

But, the more I pursued the things I thought would make me feel alive, the less alive I felt. The more I accumulated achievements, the more tired and run down I became. Plus, the more success I had in business, the more I wanted. Each time I reached a milestone, I felt that I still had more to do. The faster the business grew, the bigger I wanted it to become. So, although I had a deep yearning and desire to feel alive, my thirst could not be satiated with the professional monuments I had erected in my own mind. In the words of my dear friend Brian Carroll, I had "reached the end of myself."

How could I be doing what I had always dreamed of doing, performing so well by others' standards, and still not feel the happiness that was promised at the end of the rainbow? Why was the American Dream so damn elusive?

Origins of the American Dream

John Truslow Adams was first to put the concept of the American Dream forth in 1931 in his book, *The Epic of America*[1] in which he stated,

> The American Dream is that dream of a land in which life should be better and richer and fuller for everyone, with opportunity for each according to ability or achievement. It is a difficult dream for the European upper classes to interpret adequately, and too many of us ourselves have grown weary and mistrustful of it. It is not a dream of motor cars and high wages merely, but a dream of social order in which each man and each woman shall be able to attain to the fullest stature of which they are innately capable, and be recognized by others for what they are, regardless of the fortuitous circumstances of birth or position

The idea took hold as something that could only happen in America, and so many have looked to pursue it.

But are we missing the point? As I read the words of Adams, I wonder if we have distorted the idea of this dream over the last century or so? Have we perverted the idea of a richer, fuller life into a concept that flies in the face of what Adams described? Do we *really,* either consciously or subconsciously, believe that it is indeed only about motorcars and high wages?

---

[1] Adams, J. (1931) *The Epic of America.* Boston, MA: Little, Brown, and Co., 1931

My own father is an immigrant, coming here in 1960 as an exile of the Castro regime in Cuba. He brought little more than a suitcase, but has been the beneficiary of what he describes as a "richer and fuller" life.

I asked him to give me his perspective on the American Dream:

> I've heard it said that genuine happiness comes from having much to live for, not from having much to live on. That is true. The American Dream fulfilled for me was never about status or riches. It was and has been about a country that offered me freedom to both be and do, when as a 15-year old I arrived in the U.S. alone without my family. The freedom to be, which allowed me to watch, interact and learn from others, went a long way in helping me become a better man, husband, father, friend, and neighbor. The freedom to do allowed me to pay forward the deposits invested in my life by so many, helping me to teach and model for future family and non-family generations, and how to remember and learn from the past while living a richer and fuller life in the present.

In hearing his words, I was struck by how strongly he has embraced the words of Adams. This is what I experienced growing up. I hear this perspective so often from others, who like my father, have immigrated to the United States. It is not about "status or riches," but rather freedom and the joy of being able to experience a life lived in the present.

A number of our political leaders are certainly defining The American Dream from the lens of material accumulation and home ownership. In his speech at the National Housing Conference in June of 2017, HUD Secretary Ben Carson stated, "I worry that millennials may become a lost generation for homeownership, excluded from the American Dream."[2] In the meantime, other politicians point primarily to monetary markers such as the stock market, accumulation of wealth and the GDP as evidence that America is being made great again.

If you look up the term "American Dream" at MerriamWebsters.com it does seem we have strayed away from its original intent. It's defined here as follows:

> a happy way of living that is thought of by many Americans as something that can be achieved by anyone in the U.S. especially by working hard and becoming successful. With good jobs, a nice house, two children, and plenty of money, they believed they were living the American dream.[3]

By this definition, the way to happiness is through working hard so we can accumulate things, plenty of money and a prescribed number of children. It is a downright obsession in our society and overwhelmingly western cultural thinking. While our current society has defined The American Dream through this monetary lens, the reality is that the measuring stick of happiness, success and having enough money varies by individual.

Just today I read a LinkedIn post from an entrepreneur that said, "you can have it all!" What does that even mean? For some, "having it all" will be measured by monetary means, for others, like my father, it will be freedom, and yet for others it

---

[2] Miller, L. (2017, June 14). 2017 National Housing Conference Annual Policy Symposium. [Blog post.] Retrieved from www.nahroblog.org/2017/06/14/2017-national-housing-conference-annual-policy-symposium/

[3] The American Dream. (n.d.). Retrieved from http://www.merriam-webster.com/dictionary/the American dream

will be what brings them the most satisfaction and makes them feel completely alive. For me, "having it all" means independence, having the ability to create quality time with my loved ones and being able to live life on the terms that I want. I do not necessarily need money to "have it all!"

In his book, *The Happiness Advantage: The Seven Principles of Positive Psychology That Fuel Success and Performance at Work,* author Shawn Achor writes about our tendency to subscribe to a predefined definition of success:

> If you observe people around you, you'll find most individuals follow a formula that has been subtly or not so subtly taught to them by their schools, their company, their parents or society. That is: If you work hard, you will become successful, and once you become successful, then you'll be happy. This pattern of belief explains what most often motivates us in life. We think: If I just get that raise, or hit that next sales target, I'll be happy . . . Success first, happiness second.

He continues,

> if success causes happiness, then every employee who gets a promotion, every student who receives an acceptance letter, everyone who has ever accomplished a goal of any kind should be happy. But with each victory, our goalposts of success keep getting pushed further and further out, so that happiness gets pushed over the horizon.[4]

---

[4] Achor, S. (2010). The Happiness Advantage: The Seven Principles of Positive Psychology That Fuel Success and Performance at Work. New York: Broadway Books.

Achor goes on in his book to discuss the ground-breaking research in the field of positive psychology and neuroscience that shows that happiness is the precursor to success, not the other way around.

This is what we need to understand, yet, so many of us work tirelessly to achieve this ideal, spending an enormous amount of effort to realize this dream and yet finding that when we end up on its doorstep, the joy and happiness we expected to follow us are nowhere to be found.

Our response to this feeling is crazy. We work more and push harder. We tell ourselves that we just have not arrived yet. Just do a little more. 10X our effort. Hustle harder. It truly is the definition of insanity, to do the same thing over and over again but expect different results.

Are We Truly Happy?

If we are going to include happiness in the modern definition of the American Dream, we have to then ask a fundamental question . . . are you happy?

I am not asking a question about what material goods makes you happy, as things cannot make a person truly happy. I am talking about an inner peace, a deep-seeded joy that exists despite the ups and downs that come our way. We all search for the answer to this question, and I've uncovered some interesting theories in researching this issue.

According to the 2017 World Happiness Report, happiness in America has reduced significantly, dropping to 19th in a ranking of countries. There are a number of factors for this, but according to the report, "income per person has increased roughly three times since 1960, but measured happiness has not risen. And the situation has gotten worse in recent years: per capita GDP is still rising, but happiness is now actually falling."[5]

In looking deeper into our culture, one needs to look no further that the report titled *Stress in America: Stress and Generation Z* which is published annually by the American Psychological Association. The 2018 report shows that among Generation Z (those that come after Millennials) 77 percent state they are stressed about work and 81 percent say they are stressed about money. When applying the same two stressors to adults that span all generations 64 percent state that work and money are the leading cause of stress.[6]

But how can this be? We are seeing greater incomes, greater GDP, a growing stock market, and more and more people achieving millionaire status. We are the richest country in the history of the world and our happiness is falling to 19th place? Does not sound all too dreamy, does it?

Perhaps we need to go back further than when Adams wrote about the American Dream. Perhaps we need to go back to the founding of our country, and seek to better understand the ideals upon which it was founded. After all, if we are going to label something as American, we need to understand what the founders meant when they described in our Declaration of Independence:

---

[5] Helliwell, J., Layard, R., & Sachs, J. (2017). World Happiness Report 2017 (Rep.).

[6] American Psychological Association (2018). Stress in America: Generation Z. Stress in America™ Survey.

"The inalienable right for life, liberty and the pursuit of happiness."

While most in America certainly realize the benefit of a life and liberty that is not known in many other parts of the world, it is my experience (and the research cited above would also prove) that happiness is ever elusive.

Even so, there's something about the pursuit itself that makes chasing happiness so intriguing. The chase is a very American concept. After all, opportunity is knocking on every door in America, right? If a never-ending chase is what we see as happiness, then we must throw out the current definition.

I, along with many others have fallen prey to the idea that the American Dream is itself what will make you happy, as we doggedly pursue it through professional means. Like so many of us, I believed at one time that if I made enough money, and in so doing was able to "provide" for my family with the right stuff, the right schools, the right *everything*, that indeed, I would find that happiness, despite how much I had to work to get there. However, when those things were achieved, I found myself quite unhappy and rather unsatisfied.

So, what did those who penned our Declaration of Independence mean when they spoke of the pursuit of happiness?

In June of 2016, Laura Douglas Brown interviewed Professor Brent Strawn of Emory University's Candler School of Theology about "the pursuit of happiness"[7]. The following three

---

[7] Strawn, B., Professor. (2014, June 30). What the Declaration of Independence really means by 'pursuit of happiness' [Interview by L. D. Brown]. Emory News Center. Retrieved from https://news.emory.edu/stories/2014/06/er_pursuit_of_happiness/campus.html.

questions and answers by Strawn provide tremendous insight into this pursuit:

LDB: The Declaration of Independence guarantees the right to "life, liberty and the pursuit of happiness." What do you think the phrase "pursuit of happiness" means to most people who hear it today?

BS: I think most people think "pursuit" in that phrase means "chasing happiness" — as in the phrase "in hot pursuit." This would mean that "the pursuit of happiness" has to do with "seeking it" or "going after it" somehow.

LDB: How does this differ from what our nation's founders meant when the Declaration of Independence was written?

BS: It differs a lot! Arthur Schlesinger should be credited with pointing out in a nice little essay in 1964 that at the time of the Declaration's composition, "the pursuit of happiness" did not mean chasing or seeking it, but actually practicing happiness, the experience of happiness — not just chasing it but actually catching it, you might say.

This is demonstrated by documents that are contemporary with the Declaration, but also by the Declaration itself, in the continuation of the same sentence that contains "the pursuit of happiness" phrase. The continuation speaks of affecting people's safety and happiness. But the clearest explanation might be the Virginia Convention's Declaration of Rights, which dates to June 12, 1776, just a few weeks before July 4. The Virginia Declaration actually speaks of the "pursuing and obtaining" of happiness.

LDB: Why does this difference matter?

BS: Seeking happiness is one thing but actually obtaining it and experiencing it —practicing happiness! — is an entirely different matter. It's the difference between dreaming and reality. Remember that the pursuit of happiness, in the Declaration, is not a quest or a pastime, but "an unalienable right." Everyone has the right to actually be happy, not just try to be happy. To use a metaphor: You don't just get the chance to make the baseball team, you are guaranteed a spot. That's a very different understanding.

This sure changes things. As Professor Strawn points out, nothing in this phrase or document speaks to accumulation, wealth or prestige. Instead, it speaks to the attainment of safety and happiness! It is our right to be happy, not something we have to strive for or kill ourselves to achieve. It is ours to experience. That experience is what we choose.

Now, if you choose to experience the endless and tireless pursuit of business success, and this is what makes you happy, then by all means go for it. However, if you, like many I engage with, know that the real experience of happiness involves more than business growth, and that success is far more valuable than monetary gain, then you need to begin shaping your life, your decisions and your professional choices around that.

Choosing Happiness

I recently had the opportunity to spend time in Uganda with Beauty for Ashes Uganda, a nonprofit organization focused on the education and long-term sustainability of single mothers and widows in the Teso region of Uganda. While there, I had many opportunities to visit with these women and hear their stories. I heard stories of loss, of war, of kidnappings and abuse. In addition to hearing their stories of hardship, I learned these women also did not have what we as westerners take for granted. Many lived without running water or electricity. They had built their homes themselves from mud bricks and thatched grass for their roof. They had to farm in order to eat and for most, eating was a luxury that was not always a guarantee.

However, there in the middle of incredible pain and horror, there in the center of a lack of creature comforts was immense joy and happiness. Every village we entered greeted us with hugs and smiles. We were told how much we were loved. Their generosity and hospitality was truly humbling. It was evident by their touching outreach to us that despite the lack of material wealth goods and possessions that we take for granted in America, they made a choice to be happy. Without all the trappings of happiness as we define it here in the U.S., they had obtained it!

When speaking with several of the women from the village and some of the men who we were working with, I asked about this happiness that poured out of them. The response was the same from person to person and confirmed my belief. They said, "We choose to be happy. Despite what life has thrown our way, we are choosing to be happy." My friends in Uganda are experiencing happiness and joy daily, because they have made the choice to do just that. Why are we unable - or unwilling - to do the same?

In his interview with the Washington Post, the previously mentioned Shawn Achor states, "What's hopeful is that happiness is actually an individual choice, even in the midst of negative circumstances. It's not something our employers can give to us . . ."[8]

This was echoed in a conversation I had with Mollie Lombardi, a fellow entrepreneur who runs a research-based analytics and advisory firm and is also the founder of a nonprofit. By every definition, Mollie is successful, and has had, in her words, "an improbable career." At the age of 36, her life took a *quite* improbable turn when she was diagnosed with Parkinson's disease. It has been since her diagnosis that Mollie has started her nonprofit and an advisory firm. In our chat she told me, "The one thing we have control of is how we respond to what happens to us." In the first five minutes of my conversation with Mollie, I came to understand that Mollie chose happiness.

Now knowing this, how can we not change? How can we not come to terms with the idea that the common understanding of the American Dream is actually quite UnAmerican?

We are cultivating our businesses, our hopes of a promotion, our dream of entrepreneurship in exchange for that which will truly make us happy. If we don't change, we are headed down a dark rabbit trail.

We need a course correction.

We need to understand there is goodness in hard work, that there is satisfaction in a job well done and there is a sense of pride one should take in achievement, but we have allowed it

---

[8] Schulte, B. (2015, June 29). Do these exercises for two minutes a day and you'll immediately feel happier, researchers say. The Washington Post. Retrieved from https://www.washingtonpost.com/news/inspired-life/wp/2015/06/29/do-these-exercises-for-two-minutes-a-day-and-youll-immediately-feel-happier-researchers-say/?utm_term=.f2d458d8562c

to dominate and pervert us into a way of thinking and action that is not healthy. There is a better way. We need to learn to let go and choose contentment over continual striving. In this mindset, we can put healthy boundaries in place, and not allow work and business to be the center of all things.

This way of choosing to live in our professional lives allows us to have our goals and aspirations, without allowing that ambition to supersede our most vital relationships or our health. Most importantly, we can't let our professional aspirations be the source of our meaning.

We need to shed the idea that in order to succeed in business, we have to burn the candle at both ends, run ourselves into the ground, always be connected and leave only what is left for our relationships and health. We have to stop applauding this as "doing what it takes" or "hustling" and realize we *have the choice* to do it differently.

There is a way, one that I am experiencing, of building a business, working hard and achieving financial security while staying fit, building healthy relationships and being offline when you need to be. This is what we should be dreaming about when we think of prosperity and success as these are the things that feed our soul. We should think of the words of Peter Marshall, the former chaplain for the U.S. Senate in 1954, when he wrote, "Religious liberty to worship God according to the dictates of one's own conscience and equal opportunity for all men are the twin pillars of the American Dream."

May we find and experience that which makes us feel alive. May we make the choice to be and continually enjoy true happiness. May we not look at our business or professional pursuits as the only avenue to truly dream American as if happiness was only reserved for us anyway.

Reflection Questions:

1. What does happiness and joy look like for you?

2. Are you waiting for something or someone to make you happy, or are you choosing to be happy? If so, why?

———◆━●◆●◆●━◆———

CHAPTER 2

The Difference Between Balance and Boundaries

"Don't confuse having a career with having a life."
—Hillary Clinton

There have been countless articles written for professionals on how to achieve work-life balance that will help us get the most out of our profession and our personal lives. While many seek to achieve it, I have found very few, including myself, who actually can. The truth is, balance is not easy to achieve and in our quest for balance we are in a state of continual re-alignment.

When I think of the word "balance," my mind is drawn to the years my daughter spent as a gymnast. Watching her was a pure joy and I am still amazed at the things she could do and how she could maneuver her body in the air. However, nothing sent my heart racing with nerves like when she would perform on the balance beam. There upon a four-inch-wide beam, three feet off the ground, was my girl doing jumps and backflips, working hard to keep her head centered and her arms out perfectly balanced. Even so much as a wobble would mean a deduction in points from the judges. I thought about her spending hours upon hours of practice, falling, and getting back onto the beam to try again.

This is not unlike many of us who try and balance our career ambitions, our drive to achieve, and our businesses with our relationships, family time, and tending to our health. We try to juggle, stay balanced, and walk the proverbial beam through this life in the hopes that we do not fall or wobble. But, even world-class gymnasts at times take a wrong step and fall, and inevitably, so do we.

Unfortunately, rather than learning from these falls, many of us just jump right back on and repeat the same mistakes that led to being unbalanced in the first place. In fact, according to an article published in FastCompany, more than 70 percent of the American workforce still struggles to find a work-life balance.[9] Additional research published by Robert Half shows that 35% of U.S. workers will not take their vacation time. Of those who do, 64% will "check-in with the office while they are gone."[10] This is hardly a vacation!

Making this balancing act even harder is the always-on, always-connected culture in which we live, and the ease by which we can stay connected to work when our attention and presence should be elsewhere. Additionally, managers and employers are making it harder for workers to unplug and set their

---

[9] Lindzon, Jared. "Study Finds Work-Life Balance Could Be A Matter Of Life And Death." Fast Company, Fast Company, 21 Oct. 2016, www.fastcompany.com/3064755/study-finds-work-life-balance-could-be-a-matter-of-life-and-death

[10] Stephens, Bob. "Survey Shows One-Third of Workers Skip Vacation Time." The Colorado Springs Business Journal, 20 Dec. 2017, www.csbj.com/2017/12/20/taking-vacation-time-important-for-workers-businesses/

boundaries with demands, written or unwritten, that employees stay connected and always be available.

In her first LinkedIn post in September of 2017, Melinda Gates, Co-chair of the Bill & Melinda Gates Foundation writes the following:

> In fact, most companies are asking employees to work *more*. The American workweek has soared from less than 40 hours to nearly 50 in the time since that issue of *Fortune* was published (referring to a *Fortune* magazine published in 1949). Technology has made it harder to pull away from our jobs, and easier to wonder whether a night off or a long weekend is damaging our careers.[11]

Maybe the whole idea of work-life balance is skewed, but even more so is the new idea of "work-life blend" where we blend work into our personal lives. This looks like us taking a call when we are out with our families, interrupting important moments to "just send off an email," or checking-in with the office just to make sure all is OK in our absence. Truly, the more exceptions we make, the more the list of intrusions continues to grow.

Maybe we need to do away with the idea of balance and instead adopt the practice of establishing work-life boundaries. To do so requires us to arrive at the understanding that sacrificing ourselves, our families, our relationships and what is most important, even just a little bit, does *not* make us more successful. We owe it to ourselves to come to terms with the fact that there is

---

[11] Gates, M.. (2017, September 27). We're sending our daughters into a workplace designed for our dads [Web log post]. Retrieved from https://www.linkedin.com/pulse/were-sending-our-daughters-workplace-designed-dads-melinda-gates/

nothing balanced about being tied to our work. There is nothing balanced about always being connected and feeling more pull to our professions than to our relationships. It is time we are honest with ourselves and come to realize that no matter how much we want to strike that balance, the majority of us are failing.

This really hit home for me in March of 2016 when my wife, kids and I decided to visit friends in Florida during our kids' spring break from school. This was the first time in my career I decided not to bring my laptop with me on vacation (a fact I am not proud of). I informed my management team that I was going "off the grid," that I would not be working, and that I would be shutting off the email on my phone as well and not accepting calls. My goal was to truly and completely unplug. To be honest I felt uneasy about the whole thing and was not sure I would be able to go the full week without checking in, my ego telling me that I was too important to be disconnected from the business that long.

On the second or third day of the break, my daughter (who was a high school junior at the time) thanked me for leaving my laptop at home. While I appreciated the sentiment, I wanted to assure her that my time with them was valuable and that my intent had always been to balance my time with them and my work. So I replied with, "Thanks for that, but I always work in the morning before you guys wake up." Her reply was most telling when she said, "I know, but you spend the rest of the day thinking about the work you did in the morning."

BUSTED!

I knew she was right. While I did my best to balance, I did more than wobble; I did a faceplant as my mind was fully unbalanced. When I was not actively working I was not fully present nor completely available for my family when I should have been. While I may not have had my laptop out preparing a document for a client or working on a presentation, there was part of me (often times a large part) that was not accessible. My mind was elsewhere as I checked my phone during conversations, often stepping away from what should have been family time to "check on one more thing." Even if I was there, my thoughts were often straying to the business. Unbeknownst to me, it was readily apparent.

My family did not need a "balanced" husband and dad; they needed one that was fully engaged.

My family did not want a CEO, they wanted their dad and their husband.

They wanted all of me and they deserved nothing less.

Carving Out That Which Must Be Protected: How I Set Boundaries

This is when I began to incorporate the concept of work-life boundaries. These boundaries are clearly defined limits that make sure that when I am working, I am fully present in my work, and when I am not working, I can be fully present there in what I am doing whether it be a date with my wife, family dinner, time with my kids, family vacations, running, or being at the gym.

As is often with any new change we seek to bring into our lives, it is easier said than done. While I first aspired to live by these boundaries, I knew I had to implement some key policies in order to make them permanent.

1. Define that which you value most

What has worked for me in establishing my boundaries was first defining those things that I value most. For me, it was my relationship with my wife, Susanne, time with my kids, and my health. Additionally, I have defined those things that I believe are vital for a sustainable business and are best for my clients. Once these were clear I was able to determine the boundaries I would establish to protect them. Setting boundaries has also allowed me to have a sense of permanence. It has allowed me to have clear lines of demarcation which are not to be crossed and has enabled me to clearly articulate what is negotiable and what is not.

2. Structure and add discipline to your days

What's helped me to maintain this outlook is adding more structure and discipline to my days and making that approach known. This includes starting my work day (most days) at the same time, and having structure to my calendar. For instance, I try not to schedule meetings on Monday and Friday afternoons. I intentionally set aside weekends where I do not engage in my work. I typically leave my phone in my home office in the evenings, take planned time away from the office, and incorporate workouts and meditation into my days.

There are specific times when I will not schedule calls or take meetings, and there are days that I reserve for writing, preparing presentations, keeping other days reserved for calls. Most mornings, after my youngest son leaves for school, I start my day by having coffee with my wife and guard this time as precious. I schedule workouts into my calendar deliberately, as being healthy is important and hopefully ensures I will be around longer to cultivate the relationships in my life.

Not long ago, I shared this idea with a colleague of mine who also has broken free from the shackles of corporate and entrepreneurial expectations and she said, "That is awesome! So many of us have this idea that if we are not working tirelessly, we are lazy." Truth be told, I used to be the poster boy for that way of thinking. I held fast to the idea that if I was not at my desk by 5:00am, and working until 6:00pm, that I was mailing it in. The reality is, I am better at what I do with this structure and discipline. I am finding that my family is getting the best me possible, as are my clients.

3. Co-create your structure with others

I did not develop this structure on my own as I am far from the only one impacted by my choices. I developed it with the help of my wife and solicited input from my close friends. Now this approach is incorporated into how I live and I readily make it known to clients, partners and my close relationships. Additionally, I regularly discuss the boundaries with my wife and close friends who have insight into my work life. I do this so I can get an outside perspective on how I am doing rather than relying on myself as the only barometer of success. It's simply too easy to fall back into old habits and make excuses for doing so without additional perspective and accountability.

As you embark on this journey, you will have to determine what you value most, what you desire to protect, and what shape your boundaries will take. However, I recommend you don't go it alone. Bring spouses, friends and colleagues into this space with you and take an honest assessment of what you need to change, define your boundaries, then implement the structure and discipline. It can be done and I assure you that you will be better for it!

4. Track the positive impact

What I have found in adopting this approach is that I have less stress, improved professional performance, supportive clients, and more importantly, the space to give the best of myself to my family, to my health and at the same time, my work.

I can attest, as can my family, that I am much more engaged and present, and our relationships have deepened as a result. This past summer my daughter told me, "You have always been a good dad, but I like the one who is here now. I just wish he had not taken so long to show up." Hearing her say that was both awesome and painful. I deeply appreciated her honesty and her grace in allowing me to engage at deeper level after missing that opportunity in her earlier years, but at the same time felt a massive sense of regret for all of the time and experience that I would never be able to recapture.

The relationships I have with my clients and partners are better as well. There are very clear and defined expectations and they know when I am available I will be fully engaged and present.

I am also more efficient and effective than I have ever been in my career. There is a significant amount of research that will attest to the fact that working longer hours does not equate to better work output or productivity. In an August 2015 article in the Harvard Business Review, author Sarah Green Carmichael writes, "... the story of overwork is literally a story of diminishing returns: keep overworking, and you'll progressively work more stupidly on tasks that are increasingly meaningless."[12]

---

[12] Carmichael, S. G. (2015, August 19). The Research Is Clear: Long Hours Backfire for People and for Companies. Harvard Business Review.

5. Remember, you are replaceable

One of the most important lessons I learned in this process of establishing boundaries is that the work goes on, even if I am not there. In essence, I and everyone else are replaceable.

Read that again: We are replaceable!

This is not an insult, it is a matter of fact and many companies have continued to run and even prosper after their founders, their CEOs and key executives have gone away. Apple has continued its dominance since Steve Jobs, Southwest Airlines has continued to flourish after their founder, Herb Kelleher, before his passing in January of this year, stepped down as CEO and left the board. None of us, despite what we like to think, are indispensable!

This mantra may be helpful for you: I am not the one that makes my business go around. I am not the glue that is holding it all together. If I am, and the work machine cannot function without my continual presence, then I have built a very poorly-run company and am a horrible manager.

I learned I do not have to balance everything at once, but rather, to be an effective manager, I need to set and live with clear boundaries. Acknowledging the fact that I am not the one solely responsible for making my business world go around is a rather freeing feeling. Nothing is worse than bearing the full weight of success on your shoulders and feeling as if it is all riding on you.

Do you often feel this way? If so, I recommend you take the time to assess why you believe this, and bask in the freedom of knowing that there is a very high likelihood that it is simply not true.

6. Set expectations with your manager

Some have said this transformation is easy for me to do because I own my business, but I challenge that notion. Yes, as my own boss (so to speak) I can set my own hours, define my work cadence and keep my boundaries. However, every employee has the ability to do this as well. I know many who have (see the profile of Claire later in this book), including many of my clients who have also begun to adopt this boundary-led approach. They have shared firsthand of the benefits they are reaping and the acceptance they have received from their management.

If you embark on this path, it will mean changing things, and as with any change, it may not be easy. You may encounter a boss that has unreasonable expectations and demands that you are always connected. If that is what you desire then by all means, reply to the email, jump to respond when the text comes in at 10:30 at night, and agree to interrupt a family gathering to be on the all-too-important conference call.

But, realize that the alternative path is to take your life back and let your company know that during a defined period of time each and every week you are all theirs and will be working diligently to perform your role at the highest level. However, when you are off the clock, you are not available. This will take discipline and structure, as much for them as from you.

Here's the tough truth: If your boss or your company culture will not support your defined boundaries then I encourage you to start seeking a new job immediately.

I used to tell my team that when you reply to an email or text over the weekend or during the night when you are not technically "working" you have just told the individual to whom you responded that you are available, and you are ready to engage. At that point you cannot really fault them for taking the conversation further as you have granted them permission. However, if you do not reply until the next morning and start with a phrase such as, "I am just getting to this email," or "I just listened to your voice-mail," you are indicating that your time is your time, and you are setting a boundary. Boundaries are set in these small, everyday interactions. Ultimately, it is up to you to make sure these boundaries are not moved. It can be done with practice, discipline and others who will encourage you to make these changes.

7. Plan ahead

As I write this chapter I am 35,000 feet in the air somewhere over Kansas en route home to my family after being gone for the night in Chicago. I had a meeting with a client to present a marketing strategy for their company, which took me away from home. This does not sound like I'm taking my own advice, does it?

While from time to time I still travel (it used to be constant), I did make a point of telling this client that tomorrow I would not be available for any further discussion, and we would have to schedule something next week. While I will do some catch-up work tomorrow, the majority of the day will be free of my mobile phone and laptop so I can reconnect and make sure I am present at home. This took some planning on my part in advance of the trip, but prevents the need for apologies or feeling behind and torn between what's important, and work. This is the new approach in action.

8. Don't wait until it's too late

My final piece of advice related to boundary-setting is to do it now. Don't wait! Seriously, put this book down, get out a pen and paper and define the boundaries you need to incorporate in order to protect what you value most. Use the reflection questions at the end of this chapter. If your list is like mine, you will add to them as time goes by, but get started now. The book, like everything else, will still be here when you get back.

I am reminded of a conversation I had with a former colleague named Jason. He was a native of New Zealand and was the country manager for the software company for which we both worked. Working with Jason was one of the highlights of my three years at this company and while we did not spend a lot of time working together, I still have many stories I tell to this day about the fun we had.

One day over dinner in Auckland, we were discussing the difference between the United States and New Zealand. As Jason was never one to keep his thoughts to himself, he looked at me and said, "The biggest difference between Americans and Kiwis is this: Americans live to work and Kiwis work so that we can live." I could not have said it better myself.

Make no mistake, Jason worked hard and was recognized as one of the top leaders in the company. He consistently received promotions and accolades for the work he did from corporate executives, his colleagues and customers, but he knew where his lines were drawn and truly worked so that he could live the life he wanted.

Ask yourself:

- How many things are you trying to balance?

- Are the self-imposed demands of your business or job throwing off the equilibrium within you and causing confusion on what is most important?

- Is the desire to ascend to the next rung on the corporate ladder costing you more than it is worth?

The Cost of Engagement

I recently had an exchange with one colleague who told me that his continued drive to achieve cost him his marriage and precious time with his son. Now every job opportunity he discusses is done through the lens of opportunity cost, not just reward.

There are numerous studies that highlight the importance of an engaged workforce. I know of companies that have spent incredible amounts of money on "creating a culture of engagement" within their employee base.

What if we invested as much time and money to do the same away from work? What would it look like if we were as committed to being engaged and locked in at home? I would imagine our lives would be richer, we would be happier, and as a side benefit, our work would be better.

There are only so many hours in a day and so many days in each of our lives. It is up to us how we spend them. It is up to us if we choose to sacrifice the quantity and in so doing miss out on the opportunity to experience the quality.

May those of us who are tired of the balancing act let go and realize that continually balancing without boundaries is tiring, draining, and impossible. May we reject the idea that we should perfectly balance these worlds in which we live and keep one foot in each simultaneously, always. May we allow ourselves to be fully present in our pursuit of both relationship and work, and may we draw for ourselves new boundaries that give us the freedom of presence and full engagement.

Reflection Questions:

1. What do you value most?

2. What boundaries do you need to set in order to protect that which you value?

3. What is keeping you from setting those boundaries and abiding by them?

CHAPTER 3

Skip to the End

"Chase after the dream, don't chase after the money."
— *Old Dominion*

Early on in my career as a marketing leader at various software firms, I caught the entrepreneurial bug and knew that it was only a matter of time before I started my own business. It was during this time that I was eager to connect with other successful entrepreneurs and learn as much as I could from them. It was my desire to learn that led me to an early morning breakfast with Mark, a fourth-grade teacher from my children's school.

By anyone's notice, the breakfast was rather unremarkable. We were just two men at a table at the local bakery engaged in conversation. But, I'd been looking forward to this breakfast for a while. I was there to truly understand and gain knowledge from Mark, someone who had "been there and done that." Despite his current profession, Mark had recently found great success as an entrepreneur, living out what I believed to be his American Dream. Now he had the ability to do whatever he wanted.

In college, Mark and his associates invested $1,000 in their own entrepreneurial adventure in the form of a restaurant. One restaurant turned into two, then a chain of three, and so on, until that initial investment turned into an impressive acquisition. Thanks to hard work, and in his words, "a bit of luck," Mark made enough from the sale to choose a career as a fourth-grade teacher at a private school.

Mark was always very accessible, had no hint of ego and was one of the kindest souls I ever met. I found it most endearing that he had absolutely no air about him despite his success. While it was no surprise to me that he was willing to meet, I was still so excited to get the chance to soak in all of the knowledge and experience he could share with me about what he did to arrive at where he was. I wanted him to share the secrets of how he "made it."

During the time together, I inquired about his story. Where did he start? What did he learn? I wanted to hear all about the ups and the downs. Granted, I was not necessarily looking to start a restaurant, but I was certain there were general business principles that would apply. As he spoke, I listened with great intensity, knowing that I could perhaps do the same and in the end hit my payday.

I eventually asked him the question, "Knowing what you know now, what would you do differently?" I was ready for some mind-blowing business tip that would be the key to heading off on my own, but I was not expecting, nor really ready at that time, to truly hear what he said. Once I asked the question, he smiled, looked at me and softly stated, "I would skip to the end."

I was not sure what that meant.

"Mark," I said, "You have made enough to do what you want and you are young enough to enjoy it. Would you do it all over again if you had the chance?"

Again, with a smile and a soft response he said "no."

Before I could respond he continued by telling me all of the things he and his relationships endured as he pursued the American Dream. He described days that involved leaving the house at 3:00am to begin the day. He would get home at 10:30pm too tired to have a conversation, only to go to bed and do it all over again. He spoke of neglecting relationships and of not having the time or wherewithal to even notice. He described the physical toll this lifestyle took on him, and a list of impacts and sacrifices made in pursuit of success.

He finished by telling me how much he loved where he was now in his role as a teacher and working with young people. Being on the same schedule as his two sons, he had the time to enjoy the relationships with his kids and wife, and to engage in hobbies he enjoyed. Mark revealed that ultimately, this is what he wanted and the truth was, he did not need money to accomplish it.

"If I had to do it over . . . what I will tell you is, skip to the end."

Maybe Mark knew then what research is showing us today, that money cannot buy happiness. A 2017 Inc. article references a Princeton University study that shows, "Peoples' levels of happiness only increase as income increases up to a point, after which there are reduced benefits to happiness as you increase your income. This number is probably smaller than you think, although it depends on where you live, but it is usually between $60,000 and $80,000."[13]

---

[13] Kubler, M. (2017, August 2). Money Won't Make You Happy. Here's What Will, According to Science. Inc. Retrieved from https://www.inc.com/quora/money-wont-make-you-happy-heres-what-will-accordin.html

While some may scoff at this notion, Susanne and I often talk about how happy we were when we were first married in 1994 and collectively were making $25,000. That number was virtually cut in half the following year when we had our first child and Susanne sacrificed her career goals to stay home with our son. Despite the low income, we were incredibly happy!

While skipping to the end is great advice, much to my embarrassment I did not heed it within that moment – more on that later.

Buy or Sell?

More recently, I caught up with a close friend who was weighing the decision to sell his company. A buyer had approached him and there was a significant monetary upside if he decided to go forward with the deal. As we spoke over dinner he asked me, "What do you think?"

In response, I asked him, "What kind of life do you want to live?"

(It was my version of skipping to the end. Thanks Mark!)

After a period of silence, he eventually said, "I had never thought of that."

The truth is, until recently, I had not either. When we spoke, I was not some wise old sage, but rather someone who had since learned from my mistakes and who was trying to get my friend to think about what "skipping to the end" may look like for him.

Our conversation led to asking critical questions about the deal. Would the acquisition give them the flexibility that he and his wife desired? Would the acquiring company have expectations on him that would interfere with his relationships, his hobbies and their time as a family?

As we continued to speak, the discussion and his questions were much less about the money and far more personal, focusing inward. He spoke about the opportunity his wife would have to leave her job and pursue some of the things she wanted to do in the nonprofit world. He spoke about fulfilling a promise he made to his grandmother that he would "make good" on the support she provided to him throughout his college career. He talked about how he and his wife would travel more together.

Right there in front of me, my friend was skipping to his end. His decision was not going to be based on the number of zeros on the check he was about to receive, but about the life that he and his wife desired to live.

Rather than going back to the potential acquirer immediately, he told me he and his wife were going to go away for the weekend and discuss if this potential acquisition would enable them to live the life they wanted. Then, they would make a decision together.

Ultimately, he sold and did quite well for himself. Immediately following the sale of the company, he and his wife took a nine-day vacation. He left his laptop at home. In the days since the deal, he and his wife have dinner together consistently; he has started to pay attention to his physical health; he is giving more time to his hobbies and investing in his relationships. My friend has skipped to his end and I could not be happier for him - but the decision he made would have happened way out of context if he hadn't stopped to consider what that end truly looked like.

A Timeless Idea Whose Time Has Come

This idea is not new. Many have discovered it and live it. A friend of mine shared the following story with me, as he reviewed my draft manuscript, about a Brazilian fisherman and how he discovered what it meant to skip to the end:

There was once a businessman who was sitting by the beach in a small Brazilian village.

As he sat, he saw a Brazilian fisherman rowing a small boat towards the shore having caught quite a few big fish.

The businessman was impressed and asked the fisherman, "How long does it take you to catch so many fish?"

The fisherman replied, "Oh, just a short while."

"Then why don't you stay longer at sea and catch even more?" The businessman was astonished.

"This is enough to feed my whole family," the fisherman said.

The businessman then asked, "So, what do you do for the rest of the day?"

The fisherman replied, "Well, I usually wake up early in the morning, go out to sea and catch a few fish, then go back and play with my kids. In the afternoon, I take a nap with my wife, and when evening comes, I join my buddies in the village for a drink — we play guitar, sing and dance throughout the night."

The businessman offered a suggestion to the fisherman.

"I am a PhD in business management. I could help you to become a more successful person. From now on, you should spend more time at sea and try to catch as many fish as possible. When you have saved enough money, you could buy a bigger boat and catch even more fish. Soon you will be able to afford to buy more boats, set up your own company, your own production plant for canned food and distribution network. By then, you will have moved out of this village and to Sao Paulo, where you can set up HQ to manage your other branches."

The fisherman continues, "And after that?"

The businessman laughs heartily, "After that, you can live like a king in your own house, and when the time is right, you can go public and float your shares in the Stock Exchange, and you will be rich."

The fisherman asks, "And after that?"

The businessman says, "After that, you can finally retire, you can move to a house by the fishing village, wake up early in the morning, catch a few fish, then return home to play with kids, have a nice afternoon nap with your wife, and when evening comes, you can join your buddies for a drink, play the guitar, sing and dance throughout the night!"

The fisherman was puzzled, "Isn't that what I am doing now?"

Not all of us will be able to skip to the end with a multi-million-dollar acquisition. For some of us skipping to the end will mean making the decision to purposefully limit the growth of our businesses. For some, it means passing on a promotion in order to honor commitments made to family, as my father-in-law did numerous times during his 30-year FBI career. There were numerous times he was in line for a promotion, but rather than accept and disrupt his family and relationships, he turned them down. For others, skipping to the end means enjoying fishing, feeding your family, playing with your kids and stealing an afternoon nap with your wife.

For me, it meant leaving the firm that I started and led for eleven years in order to re-center myself and discover that what I truly wanted was the freedom and the joy I would find in skipping to the end.

Whether we are entrepreneurs or climbing the corporate ladder, we should all be asking ourselves if we are truly living the life we want and obtaining our happiness (skipping to our ends) or if we are deluding ourselves into believing that we must first achieve a certain status before we can "have it all?"

Understanding that money, title and pleasure rarely equate to fulfillment, what is the end that we as individuals need to skip to? What does obtaining happiness look like for us, and are we mistaking our current pursuits for true realization?

I believe we are, and it is costing us dearly.

In a February 2019 article, the Harvard Business Review analyzes why the pursuit of money fails to bring happiness. It states Gallup research that shows "80% of respondents did not have the time to do all they wanted to each day. This situation is so severe it could even be described as a 'famine' — a collective cultural failure to effectively manage our most precious resource, time." The author of the article goes on to state:

> Time poverty exists across all economic strata, and its effects are profound. Research shows that those who feel

time-poor experience lower levels of happiness and higher levels of anxiety, depression, and stress. They experience less joy. They laugh less. They exercise less and are less healthy. Their productivity at work is diminished. They are more likely to get divorced. And in our analysis of the Gallup survey data, my team and I even found that time stress had a stronger negative effect on happiness than being unemployed did.[14]

This is quite a price to pay.

May we be bold in defining what our end looks like. May we find that the dream we so desperately desire is there in front of us. May we give into the beckoning call to step off the ladder, step down from our own perceived importance and focus on that which is most important, and may we enjoy the ride as we skip to the end.

Reflection Questions:

1. What does it look like for you to "skip to the end" and what is holding you back from doing so?

2. Would you rather be the Brazilian fisherman or the PhD Businessman? Why?

---

[14] Whillans, A. (2019, February 8). Time for Happiness. Harvard Business Review. Retrieved from https://hbr.org/cover-story/2019/01/time-for-happiness.

CHAPTER 4

Identification, Please

"Your being alive makes worthiness your birthright."
— *Oprah Winfrey*

Why are you here? I am not asking why you are here reading this book, but why are you here on this planet? What is your purpose?

These are such loaded questions, and many of us cannot answer. It took me many years to discover my purpose, or more accurately, allow myself to identify my purpose. The reality is, too many of us define ourselves, our identity and our purpose in terms of what we do for work, not who we are. (I find this is especially true for men.)

Think about the last time you met someone new, whether it was at a dinner party, a corporate event or other social setting. How long into the conversation did it take you to ask or be asked, "So, what do you do?" In many conversations, it is often asked within the first few minutes. While it is easy to dismiss this as small talk, the fact that this question is asked so often gives perspective into what we as a society value. What's more, our answer to this question often provides great insight into how we identify.

One of my dear friends and former colleagues, Mike, demonstrated this point a number of years ago. He had just completed an interview to become the national Vice President of Sales for a software firm. As is typical for most job interviews, he was prompted with, "So Mike, tell us about yourself?"

My friend knew they were expecting him to list all of his many professional accolades, and to highlight his very successful career full of his many sales achievements. However, what they did not know is that while Mike is a very accomplished professional, he does not carry that as his identity. When asked to tell about himself, Mike began by saying, "I grew up on the south side of Chicago. My dad was a blue-collar worker." (Mike refers to his late father as the most successful man he has ever known.) "He, along with my mom, raised eight kids. I am the husband of Nan and I am the dad of Matthew," and he went on from there. He nailed it. In fact, the leader of the interview said, "Mike, we love your answer!" Needless to say, he got the job.

We are so obsessed with what we do for a living, the upward trajectory of our careers and the titles we hold on our business cards that we have used them as our primary source of self-worth and identification. We so often look to job titles and our companies to define us that it is no wonder conversations with newcomers often veer into "what do you do" quickly. This, ultimately, is code for, "How do you identify? How worthy are you?"

A recent article in Relevant Magazine highlighted this issue in an article entitled "You Need To Stop Ignoring Your Need For Rest." In it, Adam Mabry writes:

> According to the CDC (American Center for Disease Control), we Americans work more than anyone else in the Western World. Presumably, this is to pursue the American Dream. But for many of us, busyness overtakes

the dream, and, in a strange twist, becomes the way we determine who is important. [15]

This hit home for me. He could not have been more accurate. I lived this. The more I pushed, the faster I went, the busier I was, and the more important I felt. But, it was an empty promise, one that left me unfulfilled at my core. And knowing this, I realize that Mabry is right when he writes "Work is a wonderful gift, but a terrible god."

Not only does this twisted mindset impact the way we view ourselves, it begins to alter and deform the way we view others. In a recent Tweet by Grant Cardone, described as a top influencer in sales and marketing, he said, "Successful people surround themselves with over-achievers and have little time for those that don't create opportunities."

There is no doubt that from a monetary perspective, Cardone has seen success, but is this one-dimensional view of people *really* what one must have in order to achieve success? Have we arrived at a point in our modern society where we are viewing people as either those who provide opportunity, or not? Is this how any of us want to be viewed?

I Love to Fish And I am Fishing!

I am reminded of a story I once heard my father tell of my grandfather. In the 1950s my grandfather was a wealthy man in Cuba. He made his wealth by developing, along with his family, real estate along the Cuban seaside. He was also a

---

[15] Mabry, A. (2018, October 24). You Need to Stop Ignoring Your Need for Rest. RELEVANT Magazine. Retrieved from https://relevantmagazine. com/life5/you-need-to-stop-ignoring-your-need-for-rest/

well-known big-game sports fisherman; Ernest Hemingway was just one of the many celebrities who sought him out to fish for blue and black marlin.

Of course, as many Cubans experienced, it was all stolen from him by Castro's communist regime. All that he worked for was lost in an instant. My father remembers the soldiers confiscating homes, taking belongings, boats, and more and being absolutely powerless to do anything about it.

A number of years after my father fled Cuba, his mother and father followed and lived in Miami. One day, my grandfather was fishing in a humble row boat in Biscayne Bay when a friend of his rowed up in another rowboat. He began bemoaning the days gone by. With a sadness he said to my grandfather, "Look at us, we used to fish in yachts with mates and today we are reduced to row boats."

Upon hearing that, my grandfather replied, "I love to fish and I am fishing!"

No matter the status of his bank account, my grandfather did not let his wealth define who he was or the joy he was going to experience. To me, this is his legacy and one that I think of often as I did not always live up to the example that he set.

Finishing Well

I had the great opportunity to have breakfast with Andrew, my first boss, just a few days ago. Being able to sit down with someone who knew you at the beginning of your career and compare notes over more than twenty years later is a valuable experience. We were reminiscing and catching up on life when he told me of some recent organizational shifts at his company.

"We have gone through some changes and had to let a few folks go. It was amazing to me how many of them were completely devastated by the news. I believe they viewed themselves and their identity through the lens of what they did."

Andrew, too, had recognized the all-too-common trap of letting your profession identify who you are.

He confided, "I see it so often, especially in men."

We went on to discuss how both of us had fallen into a similar way of thinking during the course of our careers and now that we were out of it, how much better life was. As he spoke, you could see the joy and peace on his face and a complete contentment with who he was that was in no way connected with what position he held.

He simply told me, "I want to finish well."

Andrew was not speaking of his career or his retirement, he was speaking about his life in general. What he had come to realize is that his role as a husband, father, grandfather and friend was far more valuable than anything he would accomplish in his career.

But, what had held us both back from this eventual realization was an all-too-common foe of the modern worker.

Shame

Upon reflection, I realized what screws with our ability to define worthiness in terms of who we are compared to what we do is shame. While I am far from being a psychologist, I do know through my own story and having spoken to many others that we all battle this monster. Shame is that still, small voice that whispers in our ear that we are not worthy, that our worth is tied to our achievements, and that only as long as we keep producing, we are worthy.

Throughout the vast majority of my life and career I bought into the lie that shame whispered to me, telling me that my worth was tied to my accomplishments. This is what drove me to continually advance, make more money, get the nice house, buy better cars, and so on. (The American Dream.) If I achieved more, I had more worth.

However, what happens when your achievements hit a road-block as you're driving maximum speed?

In the summer of 2001, on a Monday morning, I was called into the office of the North American general manager of the company I was working for at the time. He did not waste time with any pleasantries and told me that my position was being eliminated, effective immediately. I was given two weeks of severance, one day of health coverage and summarily escorted out of the building. I went from being a director in a global organization and achieving much within that role (insert wor-thiness here) to being a nobody; an embarrassment.

That morning, shame did more than whisper, it roared!

I was truly defeated. Susanne and I had just built a new home closer to the office, she was seven months pregnant with our fourth child, and here I was a loser, someone who could not deliver, someone who had no worth. Much like my former boss recounted of those who he had to lay off, I was devastated.

What fed the roar of shame was my determination to keep a stiff upper lip. I believed foolishly that I had to battle on as I kept telling my wife that we would be OK and that all was good. The reality was, I was scared to death. I felt defeated, I felt less than, and I had no clue what I was going to do.

My detachment only drove a wedge between my reality and my relationship with Susanne, leaving us both to feel more alone. It is in these secret places that our shame will fester and grow and, looking back, I should have shared these feelings of defeat and shame with Susanne, as I know it would have been best for both of us to address them head-on.

In time, we did recover and it truly was a blessing in disguise on many fronts, but my story is similar to so many others, as we allow our identity and worthiness to be dictated by the ebbs and flows of business and employment.

I got so caught up in my professional accomplishments, as many do, in an effort to find myself, losing sight of the fact that I was just as worthy when I was laid off and unemployed in 2001 as I was when I was leading one of the fastest-growing, privately held companies in the country.

Shame Resilience

The beauty of life is that we are all worthy for one simple, universal reason. We have a "spark of the divine within us"[16] as Kelly Flannigan writes in his book *Loveable*. Nothing we do or do not do in the workplace will make us any more, or any less, worthy.

This was something I had to learn and, to be honest, it is still something I have not quite mastered. I look to practice what

---

[16] Flanagan, K. S. (2017). Loveable: Embracing what is truest about you, so you can truly embrace your life. Grand Rapids, MI: Zondervan

Brené Brown calls "shame resilience." This is the habit of recognizing that voice of shame (whether small or roaring) and resisting it with what is true.

I do not believe that any of us ever truly outrun shame.

There are still times I hear that voice that says, "you lost that deal because you suck" or "you are not that smart."

While in the past I would simply try to achieve more to combat that voice and, in essence, try and prove shame to be wrong, now I resist it by recognizing some fundamental truths about myself. This changes the narrative to, "I may not have performed my best in that pitch, but that does not define who I am," and, "I do not know everything, that is for sure, but it does not mean I am stupid."

The reality is, shame will come at us in different ways. It is up to us to journey to the core of ourselves and know that it is our very being, our being alive, that gives us worth. Shame can take a hike.

The Business of Shame

Perhaps I am getting a bit too Freudian in discussing shame, purpose and worthiness in a business book, however a recent study speaks to this very idea. In a Harvard Business School article, "Having No Life is the New Aspirational Lifestyle,"[17] author Michael Blanding highlights the work of Harvard

---

[17] Blanding, M. (2017, February 20). Having No Life is the New Aspirational Lifestyle. Harvard Business School Working Knowledge. Retrieved from https://hbswk.hbs.edu/item/having-no-life-is-the-new-aspirational-lifestyle

professor Anat Keinan and colleagues from Columbia and Georgetown in a 2017 study called "Conspicuous Consumption of Time: When Busyness and Lack of Leisure Time Become a Status Symbol."

The study dives into the new phenomenon of overworking becoming a status symbol, with many (from celebrities to executives on social media) showboating their busyness, bragging about their workloads and boasting their lack of leisure time.

Keinan writes, "The new conspicuous consumption is about saying, I am the scarce resource, and therefore I am valuable." In other words, only by feeling like a "scarce resource" do many of us find our purpose and feel worthy. What an exhausting way to live.

Erin Griffith, in her 2019 New York Times article, "Why Young People Are Pretending to Love Work,"[18] reveals the extent to which exhaustion is embraced across our culture, especially in Silicon Valley. She writes:

> Perhaps we've all gotten a little hungry for meaning. Participation in organized religion is falling, especially among American millennials. In San Francisco, where I live, I've noticed that the concept of productivity has taken on an almost spiritual dimension. Techies here have internalized the idea — rooted in the Protestant work ethic — that work is not something you do to get what you want; the work itself is all.

---

[18] Goldin, K. (2017, October 27). Why A Leader's Personal Values Are Essential To A Successful Brand. Forbes. Retrieved from www.forbes.com/sites/karagoldin/2017/10/27/why-a-leaders-personal-values-are-essential-to-a-successful-brand

This perversion is not only exhausting and unhealthy, it is an incubator for shame as it fosters a culture of comparison and of keeping up. God forbid if you fall the slightest bit behind or need a day off. In that case, you do not have what it takes and therefore, you are not worthy!

Purpose and "One Note"

I was speaking recently to Carla Johnson about the idea of purpose. Carla is one of the most sought-after marketing speakers worldwide, is an accomplished author, and consults with some of the world's largest brands. She helps these brands and people discover their authentic story and tell it in ways that are true for each of them. However, when she speaks about who she is, her professional accolades do not even bubble to the surface.

When she and I spoke about this topic she said, "For me, it really comes down to purpose." She went on to discuss first her purpose as an individual, her gifts and strengths and how she is in continual pursuit of learning and exploration. She continued to discuss her purpose as a mom to her children and a wife to her husband Ron. While Carla has accomplished much in terms of profession, she has realized that even without all of that, she has worth and value and it is from there she is able to define her purpose.

We all seek and desire purpose. In his 2013 article "The Power of Purpose" in Psychology Today, Dr. Steve Taylor writes, "The need for purpose is one of the defining characteristics of human beings. Human beings crave purpose, and suffer serious psychological difficulties when we don't have it. Purpose is a fundamental component of a fulfilling life."

One of the reasons a sense of purpose is so vital to our well being, according to Taylor, is because it makes us less vulnerable to what he calls "psychological discord." This is:

> The fundamental sense of unease we often experience whenever our attention isn't occupied by external things, and which can manifest itself in boredom, anxiety and depression. By focusing our attention externally, and giving us a constant source of activity to channel our mental energies into, purpose means that we spend less immersed in the associational chatter of our minds - the chatter which often triggers negative thoughts and feelings.[19]

In his aforementioned book *Loveable,*[20] Kelly Flannigan dissects the idea of worth and identity that each of us as humans struggle with:

> Last Christmas I attended a concert at my son's school of music. Early in the show, a group of boys and girls got up from the front row and gathered around a table full of handbells. One child was in a wheelchair. Several hobbled. One set of hands was twisted and gnarled. I checked the program – they were students from a music school for children with severe physical and mental disabilities. They were here to play 'Silent Night.'
>
> Slowly each child picked up one hand bell. Then their instructor faced them and pointed at the children in turn, signaling each one to play his or her note at the appointed

---

[19] Taylor, S. (2013, July 21). The Power of Purpose. Psychology Today. Retrieved from www.psychologytoday.com/us/blog/out-the-darkness/201307/the-power-purpose

[20] Flanagan, K. S. (2017). Loveable: Embracing what is truest about you, so you can truly embrace your life. Grand Rapids, MI: Zondervan

time. If a child failed to do so, she waited patiently, pointing and smiling gently until his or her note was played, and then she went onto the next child.

This, as Flannigan states, is the answer to that big question about why we are here: "to play our one note."

We are not here to lead an orchestra, march to the tune of our own band or play a key instrument in a symphony; we are all here to play one single, solitary note. And no matter how hard we strive for achievement, that note will never be played through the growth of our companies, our promotions, our professional accolades or the size of our paycheck.

We find our "one note" by tapping into our passion and understanding that we are worthy simply because we are human and carry within all of us the breath and image of the divine.

Paying the Price

Arriving at this realization was a long time coming for me and it took a long, hard journey to get there. At the peak of our company's success, within the midst of my best sales year ever, everything came crashing down for me personally and brought me to a crossroads.

While the company continued to do well and grow, the long hours and time away from my family took its toll. While I had convinced myself and told my wife repeatedly that I was indeed doing this all for them, I was on the verge of losing them as any relationship that is not tended to diligently begins to decay. While I was off chasing my identity and purpose, those who needed me most were suffering due to my absence.

This was my dark night of the soul moment, as I had to come face to face with the question of "what am I really doing all of this for?"

If I am honest: I loved the growth, the accolades, the publicity I was getting, and I loved people asking me to sign the book I had written. Why? Because it fed my ego and kept my idea of self-worth going and showed the monster shame that, dammit, I was somebody!

But it was never quite enough. There was never time to step off the treadmill, and never enough achievement to make me feel completely whole, especially when what truly mattered (my family) was suffering as a result. What I finally realized is that who I am and what I am worth was in no way tied to what I did professionally. Finally, the words of my dear friend and mentor Keith Vander Wiele rang true when he once told me in my early 20's, "I do not really think God cares what you do, I believe he cares more about how you do it."

One of my friends who has walked this road to realization is Eric. He is an accomplished enterprise sales professional, has made plenty of money, and was riding a wave of success in his career that any one of us would have been envious of. When we exchanged emails about this topic, he sent me the following note:

> The price I paid during my quota crushing years (not many mind you) was that my wife left me, taking our young son and moving in with her mom. I agreed because I thought it was temporary and I was in Q4. The thing is, she never came back, and after a year of being apart, we divorced.

> Now, every time I change jobs I am being asked, "Since you did so well at [The Company] why did you leave?" I don't tell them the above story. All I say is that it was for

personal reasons. But I am constantly reminded of the price I paid for not missing quota for 14 quarters. Most people in the world of business, especially those who appear successful, don't talk about this, but I bet many are affected.

Brian's One Note

Recently, I was sitting in a local Starbucks on a Thursday afternoon awaiting my friend Brian to arrive. I have known Brian for a number of years and this was not unlike other meetings we have had where each of us is a sounding board for the other. I had asked for this meeting as I wanted to get his feedback on a software concept I had swirling in my head. Among his many talents, Brian is a world-class applications developer and my goal was to know if he would join myself and other colleagues as we pursued our idea.

Brian and I were scheduled to meet for an hour, however the first fifty minutes of the discussion were not about the software idea, they focused on family, relationships, identity, worth and calling. This for me was quite unexpected, but as I listened to Brian speak, in his quiet tone, I knew he was onto something and I was happy to see he had figured out a good part of this long before I did.

As he spoke he said to me:

> I have realized what I have been called to. I have been called to be a dad first to my kids and a good husband to Lauren. I have been called to be available to them when I come home. I realized I have to stop trying to push things into margins that do not exist. This is where I am and I need to cherish it, embrace it and do it with my whole heart.

It was a holy moment.

In the last ten minutes of our get-together, despite knowing the futility of the ask, I went ahead anyway. I explained the concept we were working on, how I felt the market was ready for it, and told him we were looking for someone to lead the engineering of the product.

With a wry smile he replied, "Given all we just spoke about, you know I have to say no. Right now I have designed my life around my 9-5 job, I am good with that, and it is what I'm committed to."

Beyond his "no" (the best one I have ever received), I saw that my friend had done more than merely accept where he was at, but had indeed embraced it. He had come to the realization that his identity was far more than the result of his development talents, his job title or his career pathway. He had found his note!

A January 2017 article in New Scientist[21] provides insight on three ways we can explore and find our purpose. While I am sure there are more than three things we can do, I did enjoy reading these and believe they are helpful as we try and find the answer to the question of why we are here.

1. Picture your headstone

While perhaps a morbid thought, I do believe it is a worthy exercise to think about what truths we would want spoken

---

[21] Burrell, T. (2017, January 26). Three Ways to Find Your Purpose in Life and Reap the Benefits. New Scientist.

about us or written in our obituary. Would we want "loving spouse," "attentive mom/dad," "friend," "encourager," "kind?" Or, do we prefer "excellent at business," "business growth expert," "motivator of people?" The choice is ours.

2. Start doing it now

According to a study referenced in the article, having a higher sense of purpose can increase your lifespan. So, in essence, it is never too late to begin identifying who you are

3. Focus on others

The article states, "Shifting the focus to other people, whether through meditation, charitable acts or considering the impact your life will have – even once it's over – may just strengthen your purpose and let you reap its many benefits."

May we who are struggling to find ourselves grasp hold of the truth that our worthiness is tied to our inner person and not to our accomplishments, titles or accolades. May we find our "one note" and play it with all our might and strength, while continually keeping the voice of shame silent. In so doing, may we find our true purpose.

Reflection Questions:

1. From where do you draw your identification and worthiness?

2. What are some things you can do today to discover your "one note?" .

One of the things I did to answer these questions was to begin thinking and documenting what brings me joy outside of my relationships. I asked myself, "What are the things I do on a consistent basis, in both my personal and work life, that bring true joy?" After some time of reflection and looking back over my years, I realized my "one note" was helping people. This is what I am meant to do and why I am here. It does not matter if it is helping a neighbor, my family or one of my clients. My "one note" is being able to help.

CHAPTER 5

Sacrificial or Selfish?

"Real magic can never be made by offering someone else's liver. You must tear out your own, and not expect to get it back." — Peter S. Beagle, The Last Unicorn

In his 2018 book, *Rise & Grind*[22], Daymond John, founder of FUBU and of Shark Tank fame writes the following in his first chapter, "My thing is to push, to reach to grind. I get up-before the sun, some mornings-and start grinding at my goals, hard. I go to sleep - stupid late, most nights - still grinding." He continues with his grinder/hustler mentality, "And if it starts looking like the clock is going to run out on me, I work even harder."

To me the irony in these words are the ones that precede it when John writes, "This is a book about spending it [time] productively, meaningfully and purposefully."

So are we to believe that the only way to be productive and find meaning and purpose is to grind and be sleep deprived? I am

---

[22] John, D., & Paisner, D. (2018). Rise and Grind: Outperform, Outwork, and Outhustle Your Way to a More Successful and Rewarding Life. New York: Currency.

all in favor of a good work ethic and working hard at one's profession, but do believe we lose sight of the difference between sacrifice and selfishness if we just grind and hustle 24/7. Unfortunately, perpetuated by books like John's, this seems to be widely accepted in our business culture today.

I recently read a similar LinkedIn post by a connection of mine about what he believes it takes to be a successful entrepreneur and business leader. He described what he felt people should expect, and in fact need to come to terms with, if they are going to be successful.

They included some of the following:

- Long days and late nights
- Missing out on family dinners
- Absence at kids' sporting events, recitals and concerts
- Sleep deprivation
- Sacrifice

And the list went on.

As I read this, my first thought was that this is a post I would have written a number of years ago (in fact I did write one similar to this – unpacked at the end of this book in the transcript of my TEDx talk). My second thought was how far this seemed from actual success. It sounds like misery. Clearly the author and I now have two very different definitions of success.

Of all of the words that were in the post, the one that jumped off the page was the word "sacrifice." This is a word that I've used in the past, in fact I find it used often by those who are in positions of leadership and pursuing their dream of entrepreneurship.

I spoke often of the sacrifices I was making in my business pursuits. I was sacrificing time with my wife and children and missing their events while stealing time away from my relationships. I believed, like the author, that I was the one making the sacrifice to do what the business required. I had convinced myself that this is what I needed to do.

But, looking back, it would have been more honest to ask myself whether this was reality or fiction. Was I really the one making the necessary sacrifice? Or, was I just being selfish? Truthfully, during my time in the rat race, I never bothered to consider it. I believed I was the one sacrificing.

Its very definition means that when one makes a *sacrifice*, they give something up, they do not take. The one *making* the sacrifice is the one who offers themselves or something of value up for some other greater good. In that regard, I had the very nature of "sacrifice" all wrong.

What is more accurate is that my Susanne and my kids were the ones making the sacrifice. I had never asked them if they were OK with my relentless pursuits. I never had a conversation that laid out the extent of how long I'd be away from them, or all of my attention they would not get. I never once asked them if they would be willing to sacrifice this for my business success.

I assumed it, I made the decision for them, and the reality is, I was ultimately not the one who sacrificed; they were.

Stories of Sacrifice

I sat at a breakfast with a friend who was a CEO of a tech start-up, his two boys and his wife. They had come into town for a long weekend vacation. I was honored that he wanted me to meet his family as oftentimes, business and personal worlds do not intersect.

During the time together we caught up on what they did on their mini-vacation, got input from the boys on what they liked best, and like the old friends we were, let the conversation meander and flow through an array of topics.

At a lull in the discussion, I turned to my friend's wife and asked, "So how does start-up life suit you?"

While I truly did want to hear her side of things, it was immediately clear that I'd hit a nerve. As tears welled up in her eyes she muttered, "It's hard."

I felt horrible, and looking to try and recover I shot a glance to my friend only to find he was equally caught off guard by my innocuous line of questioning.

As badly as I wanted the tension and awkwardness of the situation to pass, it lingered like a heavy early morning fog. Not knowing what else to say, I looked at my friend's wife, reached forward to take hold of her hands, and simply said, "I am sure it is hard and am so sorry that I have stirred something in you as this was not my intention."

The three of us had a frank discussion about the sacrifices she was making and the toll it was taking on her and their kids; the late nights working, the travel, dealing with the obsessiveness and drive that many startup CEOs possess. I never felt that she was bitter, but rather lonely, as she had clearly given up a lot for the sake of her husband's company.

A few days later my friend and I were able to speak. I again apologized for opening a Pandora's box of emotion and found out that earlier that morning they had an argument about his business and the lack of parity between that and the family.

He confessed to me, "It is something I have to do better managing."

I understood.

We who are chasing our dreams need to come to terms with the fact that we are often not the ones that are making the true sacrifices. If those we claim to love are required to make such enormous personal offerings, at the very least we owe it to them to get their buy-in and blessing. For some, this may seem obvious. But, for many, it feels unrealistic or like some kind of fantasy proposal. Even so, I believe we must be realistic and respectful to those relationships we have established, that likely have come long before our careers and businesses. After all, they will be the only things that remain once those businesses have come and gone.

I was recently asked by a friend how to do exactly this.

The answer is simple . . . ask! Ask those who are going to sacrifice what they are willing to do, what they are OK giving in terms of time, engagement, and pace of life. Ask them if they are OK if things take a dip financially. Ask them if they will be OK with you potentially missing dinners on a regular basis, being away from home, missing concerts and sporting events, birthdays, and all the rest. Ask, and then more importantly, be ready for the answers.

If the response is no, they are not OK with that, this does not mean they are not supportive; it simply means you need to be more creative and purposeful on how you will accomplish your goals. If you ask and ignore their response, (as I am guilty of doing as more time went by) you are simply telling them that there are other, more important things on your agenda.

A Quick Trip to Austin

It was just another trip in a much longer list, and I viewed it as a quick overnight to Austin, TX, not far from my then home in Dallas. After dinner with some business colleagues and checking into my hotel, I called home and was delighted to hear the precious voice of my then three-year-old son, Luke, answer the phone.

"Daddy, are you on an airplane?" he asked.

"No buddy, I cannot talk when I am on an airplane, I am in a hotel," I chuckled

He tersely replied, "You are always in a hotel!" and hung up the phone.

While I do wish we could hang onto the honesty and purity of a three-year-old forever, in this moment, I was stunned.

I feebly tried, "...hello?" hoping that perhaps he was just being a coy toddler, but deep down, I knew he was right. At just three years old, he was just saying what the rest of the family already felt and had been hinting at in more "appropriate" ways... never as directly as this.

Enough was enough!

I called back, and this time Susanne answered the phone and apologized. But, she was not the one who needed to apologize; I was. I was the one who had neglected them, I was the one who sacrificed their time, their access to their husband and father, and took away time that I never had any right to take.

The sacrifice was theirs; for my part, I was just being selfish.

For me, this was just another day on the road for the betterment of the company in the hopes that someone would notice, add it to the list of other things I had done for the company and determine that I was deserving of a promotion. My intentions were entirely about me, as my wife and kids certainly did not care about a promotion.

My son just wanted his father at home, not in a far-off hotel room.

I wish I was able to write that this was the end of the breakneck pace, the days away from home, the long days and late nights. I wish I was able to say that it was this heart-wrenching call that woke me up and got me to see there is far more to life than a lofty career, but it wasn't.

It was indeed not long after this trip, and that very short call with my son, that I left my role in the software company to dig deeper into the world of hustle and grind and begin my first entrepreneurial venture. Early on in the business, I was home more and more present, but it did not last long. As our company's growth began to accelerate, I was completely caught up in the excitement, momentum, ego, and yes, fear of that monster shame.

I failed to establish or maintain any kind of boundaries, and my family bore the brunt of it yet again. Year after year I spent more time on the road and more hours behind the closed door of my home office. My wife and I grew apart due to my neglect, and I, like so many entrepreneurs, allowed my business and ambition to completely consume me.

If you had asked me at the time, I too would have discussed the sacrifices I was making, while it was still my family making the sacrifices without having a say in the matter. All I was doing was pursuing my professional ambition first and foremost. I was living the very definition of selfishness.

A Confession

The chapter to come will illustrate the perspective of my wife, Susanne, during this time. This is by far the hardest chapter I have written in this book, and reading hers is by far the hardest one to read. It was an emotional journey for both of us, and becomes very hard to relive the mistakes made and the pain caused.

It has been hard to journey back and relive the phone call with Luke. When I told this particular story on stage at the TEDx-CentennialParkWomen[23] event in the fall of 2018, I broke down and cried at the telling of Luke's sad revelation. Yes, in front of a room full of women. You can read my full talk at the conclusion of the book.

The vision that comes to mind as I retell my story is the wrestling I used to do with my kids when they were little. Susanne would laugh and oftentimes run the video camera. While I love those memories, I question how many of those times I missed? How much happiness did my family sacrifice? How much did I take?

---

[23] Setting Work-Life Boundaries [Video file]. (2019, January 15). Retrieved from https://www.youtube.com/watch?v=OOeFVW7g4ao&feature=youtu. be

I do not dwell on those questions now as I cannot ever get the past back, but it is a sobering thought. (There is more to come on what we want our "now" to be.)

Based on many conversations that I've had with colleagues, I realize there are so many of us who have not taken the time to look at the cost we are asking others to make in chasing our pursuits.

May you who are reading this right now take the time to assess who is truly making the sacrifice. May you have the hard conversations to determine the capacity of sacrifice within your relationships. May we all ask what can be given in order to determine what we will be able to return.

May we not make the mistake of assuming that our ambition is understood or shared by those we love. If we are going to claim sacrifice, let's at least put it in the proper context. Finally, if we fail to make the necessary adjustments, may we at least be honest with ourselves and come to terms with the fact that there is a big difference between sacrifice, and being selfish.

Reflection Questions:

1. Are you being sacrificial or selfish in your business and/or professional pursuits?

2. Who are those that are making the sacrifice so you can achieve professionally?

CHAPTER 6

A View From the Other Side

"A relationship is a negotiation but if you negotiate yourself, it is no longer a relationship. It is a prison."
—The Angry Therapist

L et me start by saying that I'm glad to have the chance to tell my side of the story. As Carlos's wife of 24 years as of writing, I commended him for publishing an honest look at the downfalls of relentlessly pursuing what we have mistakenly viewed today as The American Dream.

But, to understand the true impact and scope of what happens when good people let ambition, ego, and hustle culture take over their lives, you need to understand the impact on the people they love.

That's where my story – and that of our children - comes in.

How Does It Feel On the Other Side?

In one word: Lonely.

During the years where Carlos was gone all the time, I was a full-time working mother of four very busy kids, literally on the go from 6:00am to 11:00pm most nights.

There was no self-care, and no time for me to enjoy the things I loved. I'm not sure Carlos will fully understand what those years were like for me. Although I was not *alone*, I felt unbelievably *lonely*.

Eventually, we reached a point in which I felt entirely separate from his reality, ensconced in the responsibility of raising four children largely on my own.

"Loneliness in marriage often happens slowly, as the disconnection we feel from our spouse gradually increases over years. At some point, discussions about mutual interests, world events, and goals and dreams cease entirely and conversations become purely transactional."[24]

I came to learn that there is a real, tangible, painful and long-lasting impact to loneliness.

According to Psychology Today[25]:

> Loneliness depresses our immune system functioning, increasers inflammatory responses that put us at greater risk for cardiovascular disease, and can literally shorten our longevity. On the mental health front, loneliness puts us at

---

[24] Winch, G., Ph.D. (2013, June 28). Together but Still Lonely. Psychology Today. Retrieved from https://www.psychologytoday.com/us/blog/the-squeaky-wheel/201306/together-still-lonely

[25] Winch, G., Ph.D. (2013, June 28). Together but Still Lonely. Psychology Today. Retrieved from https://www.psychologytoday.com/us/blog/the-squeaky-wheel/201306/together-still-lonely

risk for depression and anxiety and causes us to distort our perceptions such that we view ourselves, our lives, and our relationships more negatively—which in turn, influences our behavior in damaging ways.

Damaged, I eventually lost any semblance of myself.

I lost Susanne.

I was functioning, but I had stopped living. I was merely existing – going through the motions in order to take care of my family. All the while, I was holding on to the dream that things would change, someday.

It hadn't always been this way.

We had our first child a year after we married; a little earlier than planned. We both decided that I was going to stay home with our son and any other children we had until they entered school. The plan was clear; I would put my career on hold until that day came.

Honesty, it was not a difficult choice. I was young and had not yet established a career that was important to me. I loved the 12 years I spent at home with my children, enthralled with these four little amazing humans who taught me more about love, patience and joy than I would have ever learned elsewhere.

When I was seven months pregnant with our fourth child, and our other three children were under the age of six, Carlos was laid off.

Though he was willing to pursue work both in and outside of his field in order to provide for his family, he struggled to find a job. A number of places felt he was overqualified, and would not hire him, in fear he would only leave once he found something better. While I understood, I was frustrated. Carlos just wanted to work – and I respected him for that! I just hated that I was unable to contribute to the family financially.

Since our health insurance was cut off as well, I was trying to figure out just how we were going to pay for my impending C-section. I felt a lot of unnecessary guilt over my inability to have a baby the "normal way." We were both under an enormous amount of stress, but instead of processing that together, we chose to "pull ourselves up by our bootstraps" and plow ahead.

After doing some odd jobs to make ends meet, Carlos got a job with McAfee about five months after being laid off. We were back on our feet. For about the first 18 months we lived happily and busy. He had a job he enjoyed, was home for dinner every night, and we felt as though we were living the American Dream. For me, that dream was never about money, but rather the time we spent together, our experience raising our kids, and contentment with the simple joys of life.

A Turning Point

He then took on a new role that required him to travel frequently. It was the beginning of a prolific business travel career. I know he missed us when he was gone, but I also believed there was a part of him that enjoyed the freedom from responsibility. I would be lying if I said I wasn't jealous at times. While I adore my children more than life itself, at times I felt trapped in my four walls drowning in diapers.

And worse, my best friend wasn't around to share in any of the highs or lows with me.

When that company was bought out by another, the travel increased exponentially. These weren't local quick trips. He was back and forth to Europe frequently. In fact, during one particular business quarter, he logged 11 out of 13 weeks away from home.

Those of you with kids will understand me when I say that it was actually harder when he was gone for two weeks, home for a day, then gone again. I was the one left to support the four emotional young kids left in the wake.

My husband was committed to his work, often taking calls and answering emails while he was home and on weekends, and showing an unrelenting passion for stepping up to meet his work responsibilities. I focused on raising our four kids.

His absence became my new norm. Though I was exhausted, and wished Carlos could be present for the responsibilities of the family, I was so grateful he had a job. I thought it was my job to support his career aspirations, because they were essential to our family's happiness.

These years were difficult but also a lot of fun. Upon reflection, I realize that our biggest mistake was simply our lack of communication about our needs and desires. My perspective back then was truly innocent. I chose to be content and to be grateful he had a job, knowing I was a strong, independent woman, more than capable of holding down the fort at home. I knew that travel was difficult on him and did not want to add to his burden. While my intentions were pure, I also see now that I was wrong to not share how I was feeling.

Though it meant him being away all the time, I wanted to focus on being grateful for what we had, knowing life could change at any moment.

A Glimmer of Hope

Thankfully, Carlos realized the toll this was taking, and quit to begin his first company. I was thrilled to have him home! The timing was perfect as our youngest was entering kindergarten and I had accepted a teaching job at their school. While starting a business was a risk, I had no hesitation whatsoever. I was his greatest cheerleader.

Carlos is one of the hardest workers I know. I deeply admire his work ethic and commitment to doing his job well. Yes, we were risking a lot to start this company, but it was an exciting new venture that I felt we were undertaking together.

Unfortunately, the euphoria did not last long.

He ended up travelling again, and this time it was worse. So much of that time feels like a blur to me now. I was incredibly busy working full-time and ferrying four kids around town until late at night, all in the midst of a major move. As part of the move, I left the job I loved and everyone I had known for over a decade to begin again.

I had approached Carlos many times before with ambitions I had for my career and volunteer work. In my mind, this was the deal we had made years ago. Once the kids were in school, I would pursue what was important to me in these areas. Instead, I was always brushed aside with some sort of excuse.

This began a period of time in which we simply lived two separate lives. We fell into a pattern of operating on parallel railroad tracks. Our conversations were more about logistics than anything else. When confronted with anything wrong, he found something else to blame, and made a lot of promises about "someday." He had convinced himself that he was the one making all the sacrifices.

I found myself willing to look away as he slowly descended into someone I didn't recognize, and frankly, didn't like very much.

Living on the Promise of "Someday"

We were perpetually living on that promise of "someday."

Someday we would be happy. Someday he would be home with the kids more, once he sold the business, or possibly hired more people. Someday I would have more time for myself. Someday we would return to the amazing connection we had when we were first married.

Our attitude was that Carlos had to work really hard, and we as a family would need to make all kinds of sacrifices so that *someday* we could do the things we wanted to do.

Regrettably, I lived on that promise for too many years. Life doesn't work that way – life happens now. A life well-lived is a life lived in the now.

Carlos wasn't living.

He was constantly frenetic.

He could never just sit and "be." He was restless. It seemed that he was always looking for "the next thing" without the ability to enjoy the moment.

I watched as he allowed shallow relationships to feed his ego with an insatiable appetite. I watched as he collected more and more accolades, earned more and more attention from those in his industry.

At the time, his words and actions were not in line with each other. His words told me how deeply he loved and valued me; he said that our family was the most important thing in his life. But his actions were selfish, and self-serving. I remember my bewilderment when he proudly announced that he had achieved Premier 1K status on United Airlines as well as elite status on American.

In my opinion, if you see "status" on an airline as some sort of achievement, you may want to re-evaluate some things.

It seemed Carlos was in denial – and for my part, I wasn't equipped to handle the truth.

The Illusion of the Dutiful Wife and Mother

I want to acknowledge my responsibility in all this. I always had the avenue of choice.

I chose to put up with things I didn't like. I chose to not hold him accountable in our family. I chose to stay, and be the dutiful wife and mother.

While I believe in, and have a relationship with, God – I do believe the church can actually do a disservice to women in my situation. I was so heavily influenced by the church and wanting to be a good wife and mom that I allowed it to override the way I had been raised. This has been a hard thing for me to reconcile.

I have wonderful parents who raised me to be strong, confident, and to know my self-worth. When I was growing up, my mom went back to a career she loved at some point, and my father sacrificed his ascent up the career ladder for his family. I never once felt my father was more valuable than my mom, and only witnessed their mutual love and respect for each other.

But, my experience with church-led mom groups revealed an overtly chauvinistic teaching of the subjugation of women. At first, I easily recognized it for what it was, and most definitely did not agree with it. For example, I was not allowed to keep my job at the religious institution I worked for, even if I had wanted to, after having my first child. They did not allow working mothers.

However, after we moved to a different area, the teaching of the local church was much more subtle in its narrow mindedness. The "mom groups" offered here encouraged me to become a particular type of wife and mom. It all sounds wonderful in theory; be sacrificial; give up everything in order to raise children. Whatever else I may have been interested in actually paled in comparison to the "greatest calling."

And, they reminded me, don't forget to be interested in whatever my husband was interested in. I was taught that the husband had the final say in everything. There was an undertone in their mindset that I was not as important as Carlos, and that his wants, needs and desires came first. My job was to focus on him and our family.

I didn't get out much as a young mother with four small children, and for my part, my own ego was fired up by the impression that I was doing all I was by myself without nagging or complaining.

Now, with sober eyes, I can see what I was being taught was a form of co-dependence.

I rescued Carlos from his responsibilities at home. While I believed I was doing the right thing, I wasn't. Instead of helping, I simply created an environment for him to feel unnecessary at home, and then resented him for abdicating his responsibilities.

I busied myself with very good, justifiable, and necessary things (such as taking care of our amazing children) but ultimately this was just a way of avoiding conflict. It was an excuse for not dealing with what was really going on with Carlos.

Making matters worse, we are both conflict avoiders. He runs from things, while I sweep things under the rug. We go along to get along, and we did this very well. We didn't have a horrible, tumultuous relationship. We got along quite well.

We just weren't partners anymore.

I am not blaming the church or anyone else, but rather noting the influence of such a prominent institution in our lives. The point is that no person should lose their true self, ever, for any reason.

It took a breaking point for me to wake up and begin to reclaim my self-worth.

The Breaking Point

I remember the very moment I knew our marriage was over.

He was getting ready to travel again, and I was telling him about what was going on at home. Carlos thought he knew, but it often seemed he knew nothing about the real lives of me and our four kids.

I shared that we really wanted and needed him home more.

He said "I have 25 people counting on me."

I asked about the five at home that he was responsible to, first.

He just stared blankly at me, and left.

During another weekend, we were together as a family and I watched as Carlos was on his phone, working. I asked what would happen if he didn't respond to that email right now?

He said he was a CEO. This was required of him.

Frustrated, I responded, "You must not be a very good CEO."

Hadn't he hired competent people? If he needed to be constantly engaged, checking in, helping out, was he truly doing his job well? Were his people unable to do their jobs well without him holding their hands?

He said, "You simply don't, and couldn't, understand."

In reality, I understood far more than he did.

Who Are You?

Oprah once did an interview with Stephen Colbert and his wife, Evie. She briefly mentioned his persona, "Stephen Colbert," and asked if Evie ever got them confused.

"No," she replied. "I really don't like the other guy."

Once, Stephen brought "the other guy" home when he had been working on the character.

Evie stopped him and said, "Wait. He is not invited in. Go back and come in as my husband."

I related to that example well.

I often told Carlos that I missed the real him. He was constantly stuck in this big-shot CEO persona he'd created (a version far from his true self). If he wanted to play that role with others, fine, but, I was not attracted to that person at all.

He didn't seem like the real him anymore. He was living on meaningless praise, had become arrogant, selfish, short-fused, and generally not a nice person to be around.

This wasn't the man I knew, nor the one I married. He had a steel wall around his heart. Every once in a while he'd have a moment with me where he'd confess his unhappiness; he didn't know what was wrong with him; he didn't like who he had become. But those moments would disappear as quickly as they came.

Others close to him noticed it, too, and expressed their concern. Some tried to talk to him, but in his ego-driven state, he just blamed others and the demands of his work while he sunk deeper into his self-created misery.

It got to the point where our home felt more peace when he wasn't there.

This broke my heart. He was so rigid in his denial that he ended up pushing all others away.

I recently learned that privilege can cultivate this sense of rigidity. While we are by no means uber-wealthy, we are fortunate enough to live a privileged life that enables us to live comfortably. Dr. Fran Walfish, a psychotherapist who specializes in relationships, was recently quoted in *NBC News* as saying[26]:

> I do see lower levels of 'wise reasoning style' in the upper-class and super wealthy population. The reasons for this can be attributed to a particular type of narcissism in the stratospherically rich who care more about achievements, status and how they are viewed by others rather than relationships and family. Often, these folks lack accountability and self-examination skills, which is why they consistently blame others. Privilege has endowed them with a sense of entitlement. So, interpersonally these people can be rigid, [which] in psychology is thought of as pathology; flexibility is healthy.

If flexibility is healthy, Carlos was deeply sick.

Searching for Self

I cannot fill a void I didn't create.

I understood Carlos to be a troubled soul searching for self-worth, and looking for it in all the wrong places. He had spent so many years creating a false sense of self, and what he ultimately created made him more unhappy, angry, dissatisfied, and discontent.

No amount of "more" was going to fix that, and neither could I.

---

[26] Spector, N. (2018, January 12). Why wealthy people may be less successful in love. NBC News. Retrieved from https://www.nbcnews.com/better/pop-culture/why-wealthy-people-may-be-less-successful-love-ncna837306

He played the role of the big-shot CEO, spending his money and time on people who showered him with words to feed his ego, and always wanting something in return. These relationships with zero depth (both personal and business) ultimately had no value.

The Dalai Lama states[27]:

> Sadly, many of the things that undermine our joy and happiness we create ourselves. Often it comes from the negative tendencies of the mind, emotional reactivity, or from our inability to appreciate and utilize the resources that exist within us. The suffering from a natural disaster we cannot control, but the suffering from our daily disasters we can.
>
> We create most of our suffering, so it should be logical that we also have the ability to create more joy. It simply depends on the attitudes, the perspectives, and the reactions we bring to situation and to our relationships with other people. When it comes to personal happiness there is a lot that we as individuals can do.

If you're living a similar life, it's time to realize that you're living a fantasy. Though it's easy to fall into that trap, it's so ultimately dissatisfying.

At the end of the day, when you rest your head on your pillow at night, you are tragically alone. No one knows the real you. Fear and shame have allowed you to shut out those few who deeply care about you.

---

[27] Dalai Lama (2016). The Book of Joy: Lasting Happiness in a Changing World. Cornerstone.

Taking My Life Back – After This Drink

Eventually I realized I couldn't do anything more to fix Carlos, but I could continue to work on me.

I had gotten so far away from the person I was; drowning in my own self-pity, and the growing physical and emotional distance between Carlos and I was taking its toll on me. I began, innocently enough, trying to solve my insomnia problem by enjoying a late-night drink before bed. Before long, I was enjoying the fact that alcohol made me feel good, lessened the pain and assuaged some of the loneliness. I began to rely on it.

The fact is, I am not unique or even in a minority. The "boozy mom" culture is a popular trend, with a host of items marketed to moms and even several hashtags. Kate Thayer reports for the *Chicago Tribune*[28]:

> Social media feeds are rife with memes depicting exhausted women guzzling wine in giant glasses, with phrases like, "Technically, you're not drinking alone if your kids are home." They refer to wine as "mommy juice" or to the hour of "wine o'clock" — a time that all moms apparently look forward to as a way to get through the stress of raising their children... Yet... addiction experts and those who have battled addiction themselves say the trend minimizes the dangers of drinking to excess.

This epidemic continues to rise as moms are stressed out over parenting, their jobs, their relationships, and anything else that

---

[28] Thayer, K. (2018, April 18). 'Binge drinking has become completely normalized': Has boozy mom culture gone too far? Chicago Tribune. Retrieved from https://www.chicagotribune.com/lifestyles/ct-life-moms-wine-culture-20180412-story.html

they must juggle in the ugly truth of the perversion of the American Dream.

The true tragedy is that it is treated as a joking matter. As someone who has suffered the consequences personally, I assure you, it is not. What I have found over the last several years is that this is a bigger problem than it is commonly recognized as.

An August 2017 study published in *JAMA Psychiatry* reveals that between 2002 and 2013, the number of women who demonstrated problem drinking—this includes alcohol abuse (when it causes recurrent problems) and dependence (the inability to quit)—soared by 84 percent. High-risk drinking among women increased by 58 percent over the same period.[29]

The argument over addiction is a moot point. You may not drink like an addict, chronically and compulsively but finding yourself drinking to "take the edge off" on a regular basis might indicate, like in my case, that you are merely numbing.

In early 2015 I knew I needed to do something, and began to receive counseling. Before, I had been quietly trying to survive, alone, lost and hanging onto "someday." I realized I was also creating my own misery, and chose to create joy instead. Our journey was a sneaky descent. There was nothing so glaring or obvious until the end.

Looking back, it was surprising for me to realize just how slowly this all happened.

---

[29] Ferranti-Ballem, L. (2018, November 5). Why mommy drinks: The scary truth about #WineMom. Today's Parent. Retrieved from https://www.todaysparent.com/family/parenting/why-mommy-drinks/

With counseling, I was able to make some enormous life changes. I took my life back. I said "no" to the consistent demands of everything and everyone else around me, and chose to do some things I enjoyed. During this time I was so grateful to have had a job at a school – a job I adored, with people I loved, and a teen daughter who enjoyed spending time with me. These people saved me.

In the work I was doing, I realized that I could make a choice to live the life I wanted, and if I wanted change, it would need to start with me. Andrea Miller states in her book *Radical Acceptance,* "Loosening your grip on your ego typically means letting go of fear and letting go of your need to control things. When you do this you can truly be open—to others and you a better future version of yourself."[30]

One particularly amazing summer in 2015, dubbed "the summer of Susanne," I began to speak up more and make it clear I was going to life my life, whether Carlos was part of it or not.

We tried some marriage counseling as he continued to assure me (with words) that he wanted to work things out. Once, he threw around the idea of a divorce. There was no specific reason, just that we had grown apart. (Duh.)

I remember his shock when I agreed, "Yes. We should probably just get divorced." This was the first time I took my power back in our relationship. Once I said the words out loud, I felt a weight lift off of my shoulders. I knew, in my soul, that I was worth more. Now, I wasn't afraid to say it. I could no longer be with someone who did not love or value me the way I deserved.

---

[30] Miller, A. (2017). Radical Acceptance: The Secret to Happy, Lasting Love. Atria Books.

He said he didn't really want a divorce, that he wanted to get help, and that he loved me. They were simply more words. This went on for a couple more months until I had finally had enough.

By this point, I had no interest in continuing to live this way. I was not seeing any actual change on his part – just more empty words and hollow promises. His actions demonstrated missteps that revealed dishonesty and deceit within our marriage.

The way I saw it, divorce would at least force him to spend time with our children, and maybe become a better father. Anything was better than our current rock bottom situation.

Rock Bottom

The reality of losing his family hit Carlos, hard.

When you want to question his drastic life changes, now you know why. It had to be drastic, or he was going to lose his family permanently.

I won't pretend I was excited at the thought of a failed marriage. But, I did know that I was done waiting around for life to start. I was finished waiting for the elusive "someday" that was promised. I also chose to change my perspective on the idea of what a "failed marriage" really meant. We had many great years together and four amazing kids. That is not a failure.

No more words. I made some quick and immediate changes. First, I stopped tolerating excuses for those ambitions I mentioned earlier that I had wanted to do, but that were brushed aside. No longer. They were happening.

We also decided to separate. It was important to me that he be on his own to figure things out for himself. I wanted the same opportunity for me. We had such a strange, broken, co-dependent relationship that we both needed some time and space. We worked very hard independently and together, a process I refer to as "soul scraping."

Carlos seemed clear that he wanted a future with me. I was not so sure. For me, his promises were just more words. We had many discussions about whether there would be any sort of future together, and if there was, what tangible behavior would be expected on his part.

Carlos was willing to do whatever he had to do to get his family back. He knew he had lost the most important person in his life, the only one he ever truly loved. It took losing me in order for him to appreciate what he had. A relationship in which you are loved and accepted for exactly who you are is a true gift, and should be cherished.

I'm happy to share that he now lives that out daily.

Life, Today

"To look life straight in the eye, to see its pain and to see its beauty—this is an essential part of glimpsing the way forward." - from the journal of Etty Hellesum, quoted by Father Richard Rhor.[31]

The way we operate now is based on what we both want for ourselves, our relationship, and with a mutual level of respect.

---

[31] Rohr, R., Fr. (2018, October 16). Knowledge of Good and Evil. Retrieved from https://cac.org/knowledge-of-good-and-evil-2018-10-16.

We are real. Brené Brown says "To love ourselves and support each other in the process of becoming real is perhaps the greatest single act of daring greatly."

Now, I choose to live each day with candor, and try to be the most honest version of myself. I am more "me" than I have ever been. I have more compassion for others, and am more vulnerable.

We have a new level of balance in our relationship. I am an introvert, and love being home, but I also love travelling and doing volunteer work that takes me away from home. That means Carlos needs to be home more.

I so appreciate his acknowledgement that his actions were holding me back from some of my own ambitions. He forgot that I was someone other than his wife and the mother to his children. While this wasn't intentional, he definitely took advantage of it. Now, he fully supports me and the things I love that fill my soul.

I've learned not to beat myself up. I know I was a really good mom, and I'm so proud of that. In my marriage, I did the best I could at the time. The only difference now is that I know better. What's important is that I won't repeat the patterns of the past, and I won't stay in a relationship that does, either.

I had to recognize the importance of boundaries, just like Carlos did with his clients and work demands. For a time, I really had none. I am naturally a "go with the flow" kind of person (maybe it's the California girl in me) and just rode the waves life sent my way.

Unfortunately, that approach doesn't always work.

I have enjoyed watching Carlos change and grow and to witness the outcome of his willingness to share his story and be authentic. He recently received a beautiful text from a colleague who was inspired by his new outlook. This is just one example of the kind of incredible impact he now has by being so vulnerable and open about the journey. Since he has shed his false self, he has been able to connect deeply with people struggling both personally and professionally in a way he never could before. In the past, helping others was much more about stroking his ego and making sure he felt important. Now it is truly grounded in empathy and compassion.

Advice to Others in this Situation

It IS possible to build the life you want. You have to first choose to do so.

Stop blaming others and your circumstances for where your life is right now. You have a choice, maybe not to change past events, but certainly in how you move forward. You cannot glue dust back together, but you can take the opportunity to build something new and amazing.

That's the beauty of this life.

Here are some tips for those caught up in the ego-driven hustle race:

1. Communicate with your partner

Talk about what you want and need, and become a better listener. Check in with them to see if you are both on the same page. People change and grow. What you decided early on in the relationship may not be working anymore. Remember, your words are meaningless without action.

2. LISTEN

This one is worth repeating. Learn active listening, where you fully make a conscious effort to understand what someone is really saying. Be present and responsive to your partner when talking. Listen to understand rather than defend.

3. Look for the sacrifices

The abundance of hard work you're putting into your company, your startup, or your brand means someone else is picking up your slack. Most likely, it means someone else is even sacrificing their own dreams for you. Are you okay with that? Ask yourself if you're comfortable robbing someone else of who they are meant to be, because of the false narrative that what you are doing is more important.

4. Trust the ones who matter

Those "real" people in your life love and care about you. Stop making excuses, or creating stories in order to justify your actions, and start being honest. Trust them to tell you when you've strayed from the "real" you.

5. Search for your truth

Don't be afraid to take a really hard look at your relationship and see if it is what you want and need today. Ask yourself if the decisions you make for yourself are rooted in fear or in love.

For those of you who find yourself in my shoes:

1. Know you have choices

You don't have to make those sacrifices. You can work in small ways towards the things you want to do.

2. Don't lose yourself

What fills your soul? Don't let your sacrifice become the empty promise you hang your hat on.

3. Don't beat yourself up

The past is the past. I have come to terms with mine. "When we accept the present, we can forgive and release the desire for a different past."[32]

4. Find your boundaries

What are your non-negotiables? Don't follow the words of your partner, follow the behavior.

5. Don't allow anyone else to define your self-worth

Only you can choose what makes you feel like a good person who is worthy of respect. Whether it's your career choice, your decision to stay home and raise kids, or how you choose to set your boundaries, ultimately the choice is yours.

You are loved and worth loving.

I allowed the world around me to define my own value without realizing it. While I remained out of the job market for twelve years in order to stay home and raise my kids, I don't regret it for one second. It was amazing, challenging, and those were some incredibly fun and fulfilling years! However, the choice to do so can set you back in your career.

I ended up teaching, which I loved, and credit for helping me to regain my sense of self. Later I worked in the front office

---

[32] Dalai Lama (2016). The Book of Joy: Lasting Happiness in a Changing World. Cornerstone.

of a school. Working with children is a noble and worthy profession – with crappy pay. Despite this, I should have never allowed anyone to make me feel like I was unworthy or "less than" simply based on salary alone. That's a warped way of measuring up your life, and one that feeds into the shallow hustle at the core of this book.

I take responsibility for allowing others' expectations to distort my own view of myself. I loved my jobs in education, and am proud of the work I did.

Today, I work with an incredible organization, Beauty for Ashes Uganda, which works towards long-term sustainable development and deep healing for single moms and widows in the Teso region of Uganda.

The first thing we tell them is "You are loved and worth loving."

These are women who have been told since birth they are "less than" simply by being born female; that they aren't worth educating; that their opinion is not valued and that they have nothing to contribute.

To see the radical difference that education makes to empower a woman is incredible.

There is nothing quite like watching a mama write her name for the first time, to see her selling her goods at the marketplace, writing receipts and making proper change, or to see her glow with pride as she shows us all the improvements she's made on her property for her family. I've had mamas share with me how they feel heard for the first time, and how their opinions are now valued and respected.

It's precious and life giving – and the message we send them hits close to home for me. We are all loved, and worth loving.

Beauty or Pain

"We can look back on our lives and focus on either beauty or pain. It's our choice. To focus on beauty isn't to deny the pain. It's just refusing to let it steal anything else from us." —Lysa Terkeurst

I am extremely proud of my husband.

I've been here through it all. I've watched a man come to the end of himself, then rise up out of the ashes.

Carlos could have easily chosen to continue to live a superficial, shallow, empty life. He could have never embraced vulnerability, dealt with the hard stuff, or know what true love and intimacy are.

He chose to do the hard work.

He chose to strip away his false self and to live a wholehearted life.

He chose boundaries.

Most importantly, he chose his family, and works every day to make sure we know we are the most important part of his life

If you or a loved one are in a similar situation, I hope that together you, too, can do the hard work to find peace within yourself and your relationships.

It's possible.

An Invitation

Carlos has left you with questions at the end of each chapter. I'd like to leave you with a poem that I discovered through a friend and yoga teacher. While you read it, ask yourself these questions within, and ask what kind of person you are for the people in your life?

"The Invitation" by Oriah Mountain Dreamer:

> It doesn't interest me
> what you do for a living.
> I want to know
> what you ache for
> and if you dare to dream
> of meeting your heart's longing.
>
> It doesn't interest me
> how old you are.
> I want to know
> if you will risk
> looking like a fool
> for love
> for your dream
> for the adventure of being alive.
>
> It doesn't interest me
> what planets are
> squaring your moon...
> I want to know
> if you have touched
> the centre of your own sorrow
> if you have been opened
> by life's betrayals
> or have become shrivelled and closed
> from fear of further pain.

I want to know
if you can sit with pain
mine or your own
without moving to hide it
or fade it
or fix it.

I want to know
if you can be with joy
mine or your own
if you can dance with wildness
and let the ecstasy fill you
to the tips of your fingers and toes
without cautioning us
to be careful
to be realistic
to remember the limitations
of being human.

It doesn't interest me
if the story you are telling me
is true.
I want to know if you can
disappoint another
to be true to yourself.
If you can bear
the accusation of betrayal
and not betray your own soul.
If you can be faithless
and therefore trustworthy.

I want to know if you can see Beauty
even when it is not pretty
every day.
And if you can source your own life
from its presence.

I want to know
if you can live with failure
yours and mine
and still stand at the edge of the lake
and shout to the silver of the full moon,
"Yes."

It doesn't interest me
to know where you live
or how much money you have.
I want to know if you can get up
after the night of grief and despair
weary and bruised to the bone
and do what needs to be done
to feed the children.

It doesn't interest me
who you know
or how you came to be here.
I want to know if you will stand
in the centre of the fire
with me
and not shrink back.

It doesn't interest me
where or what or with whom
you have studied.
I want to know
what sustains you
from the inside
when all else falls away.

I want to know
if you can be alone
with yourself
and if you truly like
the company you keep
in the empty moments.

CHAPTER 7

Another Brick in the Wall

"Confront the dark parts of yourself, and work to banish them with illumination and forgiveness. Your willingness to wrestle with your demons will cause your angels to sing." —*August Wilson*

On an early morning in February of 2017, I clicked "publish" on the public notice about my departure from the company I co-founded. As I sat in my home office, working on some writing, I reflected on what the story of this "next chapter" would entail.

The house was rather quiet as the kids were at school and Susanne at her place of work. I sat with a hot cup of coffee and reviewed a select passage from the announcement[33]:

> While over the last eleven years I have worked diligently for our customers and team members here at ANNUITAS, spent countless hours with clients, traveled more miles

---

[33] Hidalgo, C. (2017, February 16). Why I Decided to Leave ANNUITAS. Retrieved from https://www.linkedin.com/pulse/why-i-decided-leave-annuitas-carlos-hidalgo/

than I care to think about and been successful in building a business, it came at a cost and it was a cost that I should not have paid. It came at a cost to my family and that is a cost I am no longer willing to pay and it is with this in mind that I am moving on . . . to cultivate that which is most important to me. And while I will be staying in the industry and doing what I know, I am continually making and committed to a different list of priorities.

If someone was to ask in that moment to describe how I felt, I am not sure I could have put it into words. On one hand, I knew I had made the right choice. I still believe to this day that this was the best, and most important, professional decision I have ever made.

I was not worried about what came next or what I would do. Rather, I was excited and eager to see what was to come. Remarkably, I felt as though I had more time than I had in ages, as I considered the adjustments that this new world of mine would require.

Honestly, the best word that could describe me after I published that frank announcement is "content."

Being content is something I have felt many times since that quiet morning. Since I made the decision to live life differently, I have felt incredible satisfaction and joy. I have been able to cease striving for more and more, instead pursuing a dream with value that cannot be measured in dollar signs.

I'm reminded of one of my favorite movies, the western *Open Range* starring Robert Duvall and Kevin Costner. In the movie, Boss Spearman (Duvall) and Charlie Waite (Costner) are two cowboys who move their cattle herds from one part of the west to the other. Eventually the pair encounter a rancher who is not all to welcoming of these "free grazers." As the tensions increase between the rancher and Spearman and Waite, the townspeople are caught in the middle and slowly begin to make no secret they are not fans of the rancher, Baxter, and the stranglehold he and his crooked sheriff have on the town.

Halfway through the movie, Spearman and Waite enter a saloon and begin a conversation with one of the townspeople and his sons. The father is lamenting what his town has come to with Baxter in his position of power. When Waite recommends they could do something about it, the father quickly replies that he did not raise his sons only to be killed.

The old cowboy Waite replies, "Well you may not know this, but there are some things that gnaw at a man worse than dyin." And with that, he walks out.

It's a great scene from a fun movie, but a statement that I think of often, as I realize what was gnawing at me for years. There was my desire for success and affirmation, the resulting lack of fulfillment, the constant search for identity and an unquenchable desire to achieve without any end point. To be frank, I was miserable.

I think that if I had encountered a Charlie Waite during some of these years, he would have let me know that the reality created by what was gnawing at me was perhaps worse than dyin'. Even so, at the pace I was hustling during the hardest points of my business, I was killing myself anyway. (And for what?)

How Did You Walk Away?

During one of the slow, quiet mornings in the days that followed my departure from my agency, my phone rang. It was my friend and colleague Ian.

As long as I have known Ian he has also run his own business. Known for his expertise, Ian was a prolific writer, well respected and has been able to travel the world speaking about his craft and educating many. It was good to speak to him, and after a few minutes he revealed he had read my announcement.

He asked, "How did you do it? How did you just walk away?"

I wondered if he was waiting for some kind of life-changing insight or a seven-step plan that I applied to help guide my decision. All I could tell him was that for the majority of the months preceding my choice, I wrestled with the decision. But, once I made it, I was never more sure of anything.

I explained that while I did not have a plan or clear strategy laid out for my next move, my wife and I were united in the decision. Unlike the first time that I made such a major career choice, this time I consulted her to ensure she would be OK making sacrifices if necessary. She and I were aligned around the fact that it was time to pull the plug on this chapter in my professional life. In fact, her response had been the same response she gave the first time, "We'll do whatever we need to do."

The big difference between then and now? I listened, and truly viewed us as a partnership in this endeavor.

Ian then asked, "How did you and your wife unite around this decision?"

I confessed to him that I am a very slow learner at times, and that arriving here took many conversations and a drastic shift in my perspective of what my family really wanted and needed. What I thought was important was no longer the only thing guiding such critical, collaborative decision-making.

I told Ian how very thankful I was for such a resilient, patient wife who not only provided insight, but at the same time never pushed me to make a decision. Susanne allowed me the space and guidance to arrive on my own.

The punchline I half expected from Ian finally arrived. He wanted to do the same.

His business was going well, but he was tired, working too much, gone from home far too frequently, and he was growing weary. Ultimately, he realized he was losing his passion.

I could hear the weariness in his voice and also the tension he felt in leaving without any clarity of what was to follow. I encouraged him to take some time and think through it, to discuss with his wife, and to think with abundant freedom about what he would do next. I tried to encourage him that with his talents and experience he would do well, no matter what direction he decided to pursue.

While I couldn't make the decision for him, I knew I could give him insight into the contentment I felt about my choice. I wanted to show him there was indeed light at the end of that dark, uncertain tunnel. I shared that even though I didn't quite know how it would all come together, I was confident that it would.

As we ended the conversation I told him, "It sounds like you have one foot out the door. If that is the case, just go for it, and I will do anything I can to help."

This was the last time that Ian and I spoke about the business and the desires that he shared with me on that day. I do wonder where his thoughts are now on his business, his contentment, and his life. I wonder if he is tired, restless and still wanting out.

Perhaps it is time to give my friend a call and see where he has landed.

Sometimes the Hard Thing and the Right Thing are the Same Thing

Making the decision to hit pause, reassemble and chart a new course is not an easy thing, but for many of us it may be the right thing. It may be scary as hell, may usher in times of uncertainty, and may cause a sleepless night or two trying to construct what is next. I certainly experienced each of these things, but ultimately for me, my decision to change course brought a freedom and satisfaction that cannot truly be expressed until one has been through hell - and is now living a liberated new reality. It has brought clarity of purpose and a sense of satisfaction all without a gnawing sense of striving.

At the apex of my own crossroads, a friend told me, "You know what you need to do, you just need the courage to do it."

I had every excuse at the ready. Two of my kids were in college, and two more were ready to go. I had a reputation to maintain. What about the financial risk?

Despite all of my attempts to justify the decision to stay the course, my friend, Andrew, gave me frank and refreshing perspective when he told me, "Those are just excuses, pull the ripcord."

Was it scary to think about? Of course. However, once the decision was made, I can truly say I have never second-guessed and never looked back.

To clarify, this was not a split-second, knee-jerk decision. In reality, it was a thought that I had carried around with me for quite a long time. Unless you believe the Jerry Maguire feel-good scenes that play out in Hollywood, I would encourage you to think long and hard about your own major decision, if you're at a similar crossroads.

For me, the catalyst came down to first realizing the stress and pain I was causing in my relationships by allowing myself to be absorbed in the business. I had been so focused on superficial accolades and success to bring me contentment, not realizing that they were just another brick in a wall that is never finished and never quite big enough. My secondary motivation was the loss of the original passion and fervor I once had to lead my agency. With a small boost from my friend telling me to pull the ripcord, it was an easy choice.

Perhaps you are in the same place?

You know what you need to do; you just need the courage to do it. If that is you, may you find your courage. May you step forward, trust your instincts, follow your gut and know that there is more to pursue. May you realize that the dreams of happiness, joy and contentment are yours to live and can be realized in ways that do not require a round the clock, always-hustling lifestyle.

In the words of those at Nike – "Just Do It!"

Reflection Questions:

1. If you are at a crossroads, what steps do you need to take to make the needed changes?

2. What is keeping you from making the changes you know you need to make?

3. Who (and what relationships) are being impacted by your current situation? How do you believe your relationships would improve if you made a change to put them first?

CHAPTER 8

The Lies We Tell Ourselves

"We don't lie to protect the other person. We lie to protect ourselves from the consequences. We lie because we don't want to deal with our own feelings. We lie because we don't want things to change. Not by our hand. So a wall starts to build." —Elisa Marie Hopkins

A few weeks ago I was at one of the larger annual events in our industry. It was one I have been to for a number of years, but this year I was honored to be on the agenda as a speaker. As is often the case at industry shows, I had the opportunity to get reacquainted with colleagues I've known for a while and additionally meet some new ones. This year was no different in that regard, but there was one remarkable encounter I had with a newly-met associate that I hope was as impactful for him as it was for me.

After my session, I made my way to the speakers lounge and there spotted a colleague whom I had not seen in almost a year. She was engaged in a conversation with two others, but I approached anyway to say a quick hello. Being gracious, she introduced me to the others, and we began discussing the event.

During the course of our conversation, one of the men I had just met lamented the inconvenient timing of this conference (it had been scheduled for the week following the Labor Day holiday). He told us that he was missing his daughter's first day of high school, and that in fact this day was his wedding anniversary. He then shrugged and with a wry smile said, "What are you going to do? I have to be here."

Hearing that hurt me deeply, as I saw myself in him so clearly. In that moment, I would have done anything to help him avoid the same mistakes I made.

I do not believe he was, in any way, being arrogant or flippant. In his heart of hearts, he believed he HAD to be there. So had I, over the course of many times in my career. Seeing so much of myself in him, I took a risk even though we had just met.

I stopped him and said, "No you don't."

I could tell by his reaction that my response caught him off guard.

I went onto explain that I too once felt that way; that I convinced myself that I had to miss many "firsts" for my kids, important events and celebrations because I *had to* be somewhere. I let him know that it was a false decree, and that he could make the choice to change his perspective as I had done. I gave a quick overview of the changes I made, and reminded him that ultimately his family was (hopefully) far more important than any event would be, and that if he did *have to* be here, he could have worked with the event organizers to be scheduled later in the agenda, or be late by one day.

As much as my response caught him by surprise, his response did the same to me when he laughed a bit and said, "Easy for you to say, you must be rich!"

Now, that made *me* laugh as I am many things, but rich (in strict monetary terms) is not one of them.

I could not let it go. I didn't want to win an argument or be proven right, but I desperately wanted this new acquaintance of mine to know there was more to life than being the "scarce resource" in his career. I wanted him to avoid the mistakes I made and have his daughter's first day of high school be the last "first" of her life he would ever miss.

I said, "I'm a lot of things, but rich is not one of them. I'm just a guy who has made his share of mistakes and learned the hard way what is most important."

I do not know if my warning made an impact. I hope it did, as I knew what lay ahead for him if he did not change his perception. I hope he realized that he was deluding himself into thinking his career was more important than his responsibilities of being a dad and husband at home.

While this is but one anecdote, there are countless others. I have worked with a business leader who told me she was so glad to have FaceTime now as it was often the only time she got with her kids. I have had another CEO friend tell me about the limited time he and his wife get on the weekends due to his need to work. There is always something, always some reason, and always some falsehood we come to believe so that we can justify our behavior and excuse missing out on the true responsibilities and true joy in our lives.

The Lies

It's time to be honest about what so many of us do.

We tell these stories (they are lies) to ourselves in order to justify and rationalize the unhealthy habits and inequality in our lives. We conjure up bogus reasons to explain why. We develop excuses that enable us to live a life entirely off-balance and without any semblance of boundaries. In the process, we are made numb and oblivious to the decay of our relationships and our own personal well-being. We so often create a story in our heads that will allow us to live our off-kilter lives, but one that assuages any guilt.

I was a grand master at creating these tales and I truly believed them. Here are some of the lies I told myself and others:

1. "I'm doing this all for my family!"

This excuse is so common. I told it to myself in the course of my con game, and I hear it so often from other business leaders and entrepreneurs. We create this standard in our head that we must live up to, and in order to do so, we have to work our tails off to achieve it. We tell ourselves the sacrifices are all for our family, and that our obsession with work is what's necessary in order to provide for them.

As I addressed in previous chapters, this was a driving theme in my head. If I did not outwork others, if I did not give it all I had, then what would I be able to provide?

Susanne was right when she would say, "The very worst that would happen if you slowed down is we'd have to sell the house. That's no big deal!" She wasn't kidding either. This was, and continues to be, her outlook. The reality is, she and my kids never wanted stuff. They never demanded more from me than being a good father and a husband.

All they ever wanted was me. In fact, they were continually inviting me to be part of their lives, but the story and lie I had concocted kept me from hearing their invitations.

We often build up in our heads a false sense of what our families want and need. Many of us in business have a goal that we believe we need to achieve before we can say we've done *enough* for those who depend on us. If we are honest, oftentimes we are simply comparing ourselves to those who have more than us. We're striving against a never-ending ladder of affluence to which there is no end.

How many of us have asked our families the question of what they want or what provision looks like? How egotistical of us to make that determination for them.

I am by no means saying that one should not work hard. For me there are still times I am away from home in pursuit of hard work and delivering results for my clients. But the reality is, my family needs me more than they need my business success, my accolades, my money or my promotions. The beauty is, we can strike a balance between both worlds, and do it quite well. But, we need to be honest about the lies we're telling ourselves, first!

2. *"People are depending on me."*

This was a continual refrain when I owned my first business, and one that my ego could not soak in enough of. Of course I had to go, people needed the almighty Carlos! What on Earth would our employees do if I was not there? What would my clients think if I made the decision to not show up and rather dial in to a meeting? In truth, my absence would have been a mere blip and the show, meeting, client or project would have gone on just fine.

I was so driven by this false narrative that in one conversation with Susanne, where she stressed the need for me to be home more and more involved, my immediate response was listing all of those that were depending on me at work and how I needed to be there for them. Just writing this makes me shake my head in embarrassment and regret. What I was really telling her in that moment was that my business was more important than my family.

Did I need to be an active and present CEO? There's no doubt I did, but the 25 people who had committed to work for our company came long after the commitment I made to Susanne and my kids. Plus, they were 25 very capable professionals who I should have trusted more to meet the needs of the business without my hand-holding. Upon reflection, I realize that when my personal relationships are good and when I am tending to my spiritual, mental and emotional health, I am a better professional and would have been a better CEO.

We can define *need* however we want, but in this world, what is needed most (more than our career success) is the attention we can give to relationships and that which is life-giving to us personally.

3. *"When this all slows down…"*

It was a Monday around 4:30pm and I had just left the gym and gotten into the car when my phone rang. The effect of my run must have still been in my voice as my colleague on the line asked, "Are you ok?"

I laughed and told him I had just left the gym, and his timing was great.

He replied by saying, "I cannot wait to get back to regular workouts." I told him he could and then he said a phrase I had used on more than one occasion, "When everything begins to slow down, I will find the time."

When [x happens] then I will [desired result.]

That's the magic formula for this all-too-common lie.

Rarely, if ever, have I seen business slow down. The speed may ebb and flow from time to time, but the idea that our businesses or corporate pace will recede so we can then begin to do what is best for us is nothing more than a fantasy.

What *isn't* a fantasy is that we have a responsibility to allocate time to that which we deem important and that which we value the most. That may be a concept that many do not want to accept, but it is reality.

So many of us have spent (or continually spend) an extraordinary amount of time building what will one day fade away. In doing so, we reveal what is really important.

Are you investing more time in your business than your relationships? If so, then your actions show you deem your career as more important. If you are giving more time to your professional ambitions than you are to your complete well-being, then you are actively deciding that your whole health is not as important as your desire for professional gain.

We can try and justify this any way we like and continually tell ourselves, like I did, that when things slow down we will get back to the gym, take that trip with our significant other, or simply be able to relax. That will never happen unless we make the conscious choice to slow it down, set our own pace, make our boundaries clear, and by our actions demonstrate that which we value.

In 2017, Charlie Rose sat down with Bill Gates and Warren Buffet, two poster boys for modern business success. During the interview they were discussing the value of time. Bill Gates said, "It is not a proxy of your seriousness that you've filled every minute of your schedule." Then, Buffet chimed in by saying, "I can buy anything I want, basically, but I can't buy time."[34]

We cannot buy time. It is the ultimate limited resource. These were wise words from two very successful men who understand the value of time, and remind us that how we spend it reveals what we hold dear.

4. *"This is what is required for my standard of living."*

I spoke to a colleague just this week who told me she was wiped out. Her family had sat her down over the weekend to tell her things needed to change. "They want me home," she said, "and they told me the demands of my job were too much."

When we began to discuss options and I suggested perhaps taking a less-demanding role, she said, "Well, my pay is important!"

I asked her if it was more important than her relationship with her kids and her husband. Soon I realized that a lie about the

[34] Rose, C. (2017, January 1). Bill Gates and Warren Buffett. Retrieved from https://charlierose.com/videos/29774

true value of her salary was entrapping her, and potentially keeping her in a personally destructive job.

Why do we allow the allure of money to entrap us? What is it that makes us think we need to have more and that this is what's most important? Perhaps that is the default attitude in a capitalist society such as ours. Still, I am struck by the fact that most who will read this book drive two cars, are able to eat out more than once per month, have taken vacations and live good lives. These facts alone mean you are in the top 10 percent of the wealthiest people in the world.

A friend once saw a "God Bless America" bumper sticker and said to me, "I think he already has."

With that perspective, ask yourself: Is this really what it is all about?

I am not at all advocating for being destitute or being irresponsible in not supporting our families, but let us not fall prey to thinking that it is healthy to reject the pleas of our families and their desire for a quality life with us in exchange for a few extra dollars.

When I co-founded my first company, I remember a conversation with Susanne about what we would need to "sacrifice" in order to give it a go. I began talking about cutting back on the number of times per month we took the family out to eat, and taking fewer Starbucks runs.

She responded, "Those will not be sacrifices, those are nice-to-haves."

She was 100% right and I firmly believe we as a society have confused the two.

If we are willing and honest with ourselves, many of us could add up our "nice-to-haves" and see that we spend a lot on fluff. Isn't a whole-hearted existence far more important?

Are These Lies Worth It?

I'm sure if I spent more time thinking through the past, I could detail a number of other lies I convinced myself were true. Perhaps you resonate with some of these, or have some of your own that are not listed, and you still truly believe them.

Whatever the circumstance, ask yourself: Is it worth it to uphold these lies?

Is it worth missing a first day of high school for your daughter, or a baseball playoff game that's important to your son? Is it worth missing a recital, a string of family dinners alongside your spouse, playing a video game with your son or wrestling on the floor and being flooded with the laughter of your children? Is it worth sacrificing the chance to consistently kiss them good night?

I would hope the answer is a resounding no!

While there was plenty I missed, I have made the choice that I will no longer. I now block these things in my calendar. I call them "the immovables." These things include breaks in the school calendar such as fall break, first days of school, concerts, special events, birthdays, long weekends, and similar opportunities to be together as a family. I have made the choice, with the help of some, to reject the lies I told myself for years. There are times when I miss an industry event, a call, or meeting and life moves on.

I am better for it and no longer have to bargain with my guilt.

I recently had to take a late call with a client that started at 6:30pm local time here in Colorado (Susanne and I had discussed the moving of this boundary before I committed.) The call was scheduled for 90 minutes and I had told Susanne and my son Luke (the youngest who is still in high school) that after the call we should go get some ice cream. With 20 minutes left on the call, I reminded my client that I had a hard stop in 20 minutes and asked if there were any last-minute items we should address. Later that week I was with the client who told me she respected my commitment to the timeframe. I smiled and asked her if she wanted to know what the hard stop was for? She nodded, and when I told her it was a promised ice cream with my wife and son, she laughed and said "that's awesome!"

I couldn't have agreed more.

It's Truly Possible

I know what some of you may be thinking. Perhaps you feel the same as my new colleague did, thinking it's easy for me to say this because <insert rationalization here>.

But is it? I know that some of the stories I have recounted were of friends who really did hit the jackpot, but that's just not been my story. Yet, I was still able to walk away, change course and live my life in the now.

As my friend Andrew told me when I discussed this with him, anything keeping me from pulling the ripcord was just an excuse, and another lie that kept me running on the hamster wheel of futility.

So, what lies do you believe? If you really want to get to some of these answers, I challenge you to ask a close friend, spouse or your kids. Ask them:

- What version of your "truth" do they see?

- What lies that have you mistaken for truth?

- What parts of you are they not getting?

Fair warning to you: If you heed my advice, you may not like the answers, but at least you will get an honest and fair perspective. This is hard work, but it's important work.

May we who have believed certain lies and convinced ourselves of the things that rob us and our loved ones of beauty, connection and experience, reject them. May we free ourselves from the entrapment of the lies that we allow into our lives because of what society says. May we embrace what is true and in so doing find the joy in the freedom of being present.

Reflection Questions:

1. What lies do you tell yourself that keep you from experiencing the best of your relationships and your life?

2. What lies would those around you say you believe?

3. Is your definition of success an obstacle to experiencing the best your life has to offer?

4. Are you putting more time into superficial things than those things that are life-giving? If so, what are those things and what would change if you gave less of yourself to them?

CHAPTER 9

The Destruction of (Hustle) Porn

"Be OK with being happier instead of being a hustler."
—*Erica Douglass*

A friend of ours recently shared this illustration from artist and author Adam J. Kurtz on Instagram:[35]

 adamjk   ...

DO WHAT YoU LOVE
AND You'LL ~~NEVER~~
~~WORK A DAY IN YOUR~~
~~LIFE~~ WORK SUPER
FUCKING HARD ALL
THE TIME WITH NO
SEPARATION OR ANY
BOUNDARIES AND ALSO
TAKE EVERYTHING
EXTREMELY PERSONALLY
@ADAMJK

---

[35] Kurtz, Adam [@AdamJK]. (2019, March 23). [Photo of illustration.] Retrieved from www.instagram.com/p/BvXHptGAOF5

The image had gone a bit viral and become a meme, because I think it struck true to so many of us who had once fallen victim to the hustle of "doing what we love." It's so easy to get caught up in our work identity with no boundaries, to the point that we take everything personally and lose any semblance of work-life balance.

When I read this meme, my mind was drawn to a quote from Brené Brown that I used in my TEDx speech (the full transcript of which is included at the end of the book). She says, "If we want to live a wholehearted life, we must be intentional about cultivating sleep and play, and about letting go of exhaustion as a status symbol and productivity as self-worth."

There is nothing noble about tying your identity to your work, no matter how noble the cause. There is nothing wholehearted about living a life with no boundaries or separation and there is nothing attractive about taking everything so personally that it stunts your ability to grow both personally and professionally. The dangerous truth revealed in this illustration is a sober perspective of real sacrifices made in our pursuit of the hustle.

The fantasy of "hustle" is a dangerous trend that is seeping into the minds of entrepreneurs and business leaders alike. We see industry articles, entrepreneurs on social media, and TV personalities all lauding the grind and the pursuit of success at the expense of all else. This has become known as "hustle porn."

In hustle porn, like that meme illustrates, unless you are willing to leave everything else behind (family, sleep, exercise, relationships, etc.) and put the business ahead of all else, you will not be successful. You are weak. You are not trying hard enough. You are a failure, even if by all other measures, you're doing well.

I bet few business leaders who embody this warped view of "business above all else" (and boast about their long hours online) would *actually* come right out and use the term "hustle porn," but they embody it quite well. There is a long list that advocate for this way of thinking and living.

In a recent interview with *CNBC's Make It*, Kevin O'Leary of *Shark Tank* fame said:

> If I have to give one piece of advice to someone who's thinking about starting a business, I tell them this: Forget about balance. You're going to work 25 hours a day, seven days a week, forever. That's what it takes to be successful. You're going to be competing with tons of determined people who want to kick your ass. It's a job 24-7 job. Get over it, and get ready for it.[36]

There is no doubt that O'Leary has made more money than most, but is this the only way to "success?" Is this the definition of the American Dream? Is this what will bring fulfillment and happiness? What about burnout? What about balance? This is "hustle porn" on full display, and countless entrepreneurs and business leaders accept this dangerous advice at face value.

Another "self-made millionaire," the previously mentioned Grant Cardone also ascribes to this idea that in order to "succeed" (defined as being a millionaire) you have to be willing to

---

[36] Berger, S. (2018, November 14). Kevin O'Leary: If you want to get rich, start working 25 hours a day, 7 days a week. CNBC. Retrieved from https://www.cnbc.com/2018/11/14/kevin-oleary-says-entrepreneurs-work-25-hours-a-day-7-days-a-week.html

work 95 hours per week rather than the 9-5.[37] This means, if money is your measure of success, and you believe Cardone, then you must be willing to devote more than 56% of your life to work in order to be successful. Take that further and consider the math. Even if you worked every day of the week, with no weekends, with an average of 8 hours of sleep per night, you have 112 total waking hours each week. Working 95 hours a week means we must sacrifice 85% of our waking hours to work under this mindset. That number jumps to 112% if you, God forbid, took a break on weekends but followed Cardone's ridiculous advice. What kind of dream is this?

This story is, frankly, getting old. And, many are starting to push back against the individuals promoting hustle porn and getting swept up in the trend. I'm so encouraged by the voices that are speaking out against it, and personally hope this chapter and the entirety of the book do that as well.

In a recent article published in *Quartz at Work*,[38] Alexis Ohanian, co-founder of Reddit, is quoted as follows, "The idea that unless you are suffering, grinding, working every hour of every day, you're not working hard enough . . . this is one of the most toxic, dangerous things in tech right now." (I would say it's infiltrated the culture around all business and entrepreneurship.) Ohanian continues by saying, "It's such bullshit, utter

---

[37] Elkins, K. (2016, December 5). Self-made millionaire: If you want to get rich, start working 95 hours a week. Self-made Millionaire: If You Want to Get Rich, Start Working 95 Hours a Week. Retrieved from https://www.cnbc.com/2016/12/05/self-made-millionaire-if-you-want-to-get-rich-start-working-95-hours-a-week.html

[38] Fessler, L. (2018, November 10). Reddit co-founder Alexis Ohanian is taking a stand against "hustle porn". Retrieved from https://qz.com/work/1458073/reddit-co-founder-alexis-ohanian-is-taking-a-stand-against-hustle-porn/

bullshit, it has a deleterious effect not just on your business, but on your well-being."

Perhaps this is just one man's opinion, but I do believe he is onto something, as do medical studies. According to the University of Pennsylvania, "subjects who were limited to only 4.5 hours of sleep a night for one week reported feeling more stressed, angry, sad, and mentally exhausted." How can any of these things be good for your business?

The truth is, I used to subscribe to these lies and was bound and determined to outwork and out-hustle others in my industry. I also falsely believed that by doing this, it would lead to "success," as defined by a big fat dollar sign.

I realized the hard way that this is not sustainable and certainly not a healthy definition of success. As the Quartz article states "remember: like most porn, hustle porn is not a valid representation of reality." It is not realistic, a complete fantasy, and one that is utterly destructive.

How to Break the Illusion of Hustle Porn

Make no mistake, I work hard and I enjoy the work I do. Given my new approach to work-life boundaries, I know that not only am I working hard, I am working smarter, with so much more efficiency and mental clarity. When I survey all aspects of my life, I am at the most successful point of my career. I am achieving this without selling my soul, with 8-9 hours of sleep per night, with regular exercise and with more time spent with my wife and family.

Don't fall into the trap of thinking it is easy for the wealthy co-founder of Reddit to state such things. That's an excuse.

Take my word for it, the word of someone who is not monetarily wealthy but completely fulfilled. IT CAN BE DONE!

Breaking the illusion of "hustle porn" first requires us to think critically about the advice of these public figures who are promoting an entirely unrealistic lifestyle. Let's stop sharing their LinkedIn status updates, liking their Instagram photos, booking them to speak at industry events on this topic, and stop celebrating their egotistical calls for attention each time they boast about long hours and sleepless nights in pursuit of the hustle. There is nothing here to be lauded or praised as when we do so, we are only condoning an unhealthy approach to life and business.

We must remember that not only is this mindset dangerous to individuals who sacrifice their well-being, but it also creates an incredibly unfair business culture. As Ohanian states in that same article, "hustle porn" reinforces "sexist stereotypes that to win in tech, you have to ditch everything outside of work and devote your life to your company, a tradeoff many people (and women especially) simply cannot make."

We need to get real, and create a better goal for ourselves and our industries. The most important step in arriving there is looking at how we define success.

I have come to a place of clarity for me in which I define success much differently than I had for the majority of my life. While there is nothing wrong with making good money, having stuff and achieving millionaire status, I do believe it is dangerous to use this as a barometer for success.

I know far too many people who have more money than they could ever know what to do with, yet are miserable and void of joy. This isn't success. This is simply an accumulation of wealth, and the two are vastly different.

In looking at my life now, I can say with 100 percent honesty that I do not want for anything, love the life I live, have stronger relationships, and better mental, emotional, spiritual and physical health than I have ever had before. I guess you could say I am wildly successful!

Of course there are days you need to hustle, work hard, and at times put in long hours to ensure things get done. I do not think it is realistic to think this will never happen. However, what is *not* realistic or healthy is to accept and design a life around the false promise of millionaire status. Doing this day in and day out, as O'Leary recommends, at the expense of what *life is really about,* is unreasonable, irresponsible, and as Ohanian states, toxic.

Enough with "hustle porn."

May you reject the idea that success is only found in the pursuit, exhaustion and a lack of self-care. May you find success and wholeheartedness in all aspects of your life, and reject the notion that your business and career are what matters most. May you, and all aspiring leaders, look up to entrepreneurs and business leaders who demonstrate work/life balance and boundaries. May you never fall victim to the fantasy of "hustle porn."

Reflection Questions:

1. Would you rather be known as being happier or being a hustler? Why? Ask your loved ones to answer this about you.

2. What are you cultivating today that is keeping you from living a wholehearted life?

3. How do you define "success?".

CHAPTER 10

Are You Living Your Values?

"When you live according to your values you live authentically." —Anonymous

All of us have certain values we live by. We hold these beliefs that guide and define our choices, impact our decisions and are fundamental to who we are. However, if we do not consistently tend to ourselves, we can find over time that we have strayed far from our values, and are suddenly in a place we could have never imagined.

In looking back on the years I spent in my unhinged business pursuits, I realize that I was not cultivating that which was healthy, and as a result found myself far away from the values I once said were fundamental to who I was. At the time, I would have never admitted this out loud. It was largely unconscious, but over time I traded in my core values for the pursuit of all things that were so called "American."

If, during this time, you had asked me what my core values were, I would have rattled off a list that included a spiritual pursuit and relationship with God and a family-first approach that meant they would always come first. I would have told you that I fundamentally believed in integrity in everything I did, authenticity and hard work.

But did I?

While it is hard to admit, what I said and what I practiced could not have been more fundamentally different. I had deluded myself into thinking I was still living my core values, when in reality, I had drifted farther from them.

In looking back, I was merely giving lip service to all the values I once said were most important. I was simply all talk and no action, and as the saying goes, "talk is cheap." My spiritual life became quite stale, and in fact became more of an afterthought than anything. I would still speak to it if asked, but did not actively tend to it or lean into it for any source of strength or inspiration. As for my family-first approach, I was never home, I was hardly available when I was home in any meaningful way, and I was often irritable and mentally and emotionally removed. So, despite what words I said out loud, the reality was that my interests and pursuits were first. My family was consistently taking a back seat.

As for integrity, yes, I did right by my partners, my employees and clients, but fundamentally I was not being truthful with myself or those around me. Honestly, my relationships were in shambles. I was not willing to be authentic with others, I was not true to my marriage and I had created a fabrication in my own mind about who I was and the importance of what I was building.

What happened? I was not trying consciously to trample on my values. I did not one day wake up and decide that my values served no purpose and therefore should change. In fact, the process was slow. Over time, the pursuit of my ambitions led to an erosion of all I held close. As with anything, if you do not continually tend to it, rot sets in. I found this to be true of both my values and core convictions. Much to my regret, they became stale and I stopped following them as the kind of guiding force in my life they were intended to be. It was a steady but methodical deconstruction that occurred such that I hardly noticed as it was happening until one day, I hit rock bottom.

I found myself soberly looking at my life, and wondering how in the world I had arrived there. That's how it happens.

I know others who have had the same experience. When asked for the monumental event or decision that changed everything, their response is more often than not, "It was not just one thing, but rather a whole bunch of little things and choices over time. One day I woke up and realized how far I'd strayed from where I was."

Living With Your Whole Heart

I was discussing this disconnect with Michelle, a colleague and friend who experienced something very similar in her professional career. While her story is a bit different from mine (all of our stories are unique), it reveals how easy it is to slide into a place of complacency where we say one thing but are fundamentally living another. Oftentimes we need a wake-up call to jar us back into the reality of what is true and important.

Here is Michelle's story:

> A few years ago, I was hired at a Fortune 50 company as a Vice President. I thought I had finally arrived. Me, the kid from a blue-collar town that was more famous for its nearby airport than anything else, had become a Vice

President. I had an organization of 125, a budget beyond my wildest dreams, and the deference of others within the company when they greeted me due to my title.

Yes, I had made it!

I set about "proving" that I both belonged and deserved to be there. Within weeks of arriving, I was often one of the first employees in and one of the last people to leave the office. I figured it was just because I had so much to learn and eventually the pace would be manageable. Every night I would promise my husband that "Tonight is different, I'll leave on time." Some nights I would keep that promise, but on most evenings, there was another crisis, another fire drill, and another case of "just one more thing to do before I leave the office."

I became familiar with apologizing as I walked in the door.

I would leave home as my two young kids were just getting up (or still sleeping) and get home just in time to have an hour with them before their bedtime around 8:00pm.

After I put the kids to bed I immediately would fall into bed myself, exhausted, with nothing left to give. Most days I would wake up at 4:30am or earlier so I could "catch up" on work prior to working out. We had a high-ranking executive who often sent emails at 4:00am, and I was proud that I responded almost as soon as he sent one of these notes, as if it was a competition to see who was working harder.

I didn't work every weekend, but it happened far more than I'd like to admit. I would tell my kids and husband that I only had "1-2 hours of work," but before I knew it, the day would be gone. On those days, my husband often took the kids out to give me time and space. While this was super thoughtful of him, I missed days at the zoo, bike rides around the neighborhood, and lounging by the pool. When I did join them, if I had been working just prior, I was often distracted and not totally present.

In addition to the hours commuting, staying late or working during off-hours, I also traveled regularly. This heavy travel schedule let me "achieve" Southwest A-List status (requiring 25 flights) within months of my first year on the job. When I traveled, I was diligent about video-calling home with FaceTime, but if I'm honest, I didn't spend enough time really listening to my kids talk about their days. I was preoccupied with getting back to a business dinner or completing a presentation before heading to bed.

I justified all of this by telling myself that I needed to make a good impression on the executives at my new job, and in doing so I would reap further rewards. I would also tell myself that I'd catch up with my family "when things calmed down." However, as many of us know, there is always one more "to do" once you start prioritizing your work over other things like relationships and your family.

In an effort to become even more effective at work, I began working with a coach so that I could improve my "brand" at my organization. Here, the only way to get things done was through, and with, other people. I thought if I could get more accomplished, faster, it would allow me to take a bit more time for my family and myself.

The coach I worked with was amazing. As a first step, she recommended that I complete a 360° evaluation, getting reviews of my work and how people perceived me from a wide range of individuals throughout the organization from my direct boss to peers and direct reports.

As we walked through my 360°, she showed me evidence that I actually didn't have a brand problem. In fact, my 360° was largely favorable with most feedback focused on my need to "speak up more." My coach noted that the results indicated I was doing something right and already had the ability to build bridges and achieve milestones with, and through, my colleagues.

We continued to meet over the course of six months as I still thought there were areas I could improve. I thought if I was just a bit more effective, I could achieve more. However, at every other meeting I'd arrive exhausted, distracted and not entirely present for our discussion.

Finally, we were coming to the end of our six-month engagement. I was no further in my "brand" work, and had I arrived for our last session as I usually did; with my mind elsewhere. As we were talking about what we should *really* focus on in our work together, and whether or not we should even continue our engagement, she stopped me, looked me dead in the eyes and said, "Can I be really, brutally honest with you and ask you a question?"

I said yes, of course, as I am always one for direct communication.

She then asked "Are you living your values at your current job?"

I, who never publicly show much emotion, teared up immediately and answered with equal honesty, "No, this isn't the life I want. I keep trying to convince myself that if I just work a little harder and keep pushing, that there'll be a payoff of more time with my family. But, that isn't happening. I'm missing out on things that are important to me and I can't seem to get it right."

She continued to ask more questions, and I explained that I felt like I was failing as a parent as I wasn't able to be present (both mentally and physically) with my kids. I also admitted I was worried about my marriage as I saw my husband even less than our children, with both of us relying more and more on our nanny (something we promised each other we would never do).

My coach then asked me to think of when I was the happiest in a job, and what it would take for me to find that happiness again. She asked me to visualize what it would look like for me personally, for my kids, and for my husband. This simple line of questioning began for me a journey that ultimately led me to leave my role and find another opportunity.

I'm happy to share that I have found a new role, and it is one that affords me what I truly want: quality time with my kids and husband. It is one that I took because of, and at the same time recommitted to, the core values that I believe in.

Besides my new job, we've made some shifts at home as well. One of the changes my husband and I made was to let go of our nanny, giving us an opportunity to "figure out" childcare, soccer practices and other activities in a way that would work for both of us. As part of this, we recommitted to not travel at the same time, something that was easy to be more relaxed about when we had the resources of a nanny to cover an occasional overnight.

I now walk or cycle my youngest to and from school. We participate in various carpools to get the kids back and forth to soccer practices, and their activities have the same preference in our calendars as weekly business-related meetings. I still travel, but when I do, I make sure that my kids are the ones who end our FaceTimes. I also keep my travel to a minimum, always choosing to take a same-day, later flight when possible so I'm home when they wake up. When I'm home, I'm not on my computer or phone. I'm looking directly into their eyes as they speak to me. I'm not only happier and more fulfilled, but even my kids have remarked, "You're different than you used to be."

I was so touched by Michelle's story, but there is more to it.

Since her departure from the old job to the new one, Michelle received a diagnosis of cancer and shared with me:

Cancer made me focus on the "extraordinary ordinary day." I now can say I am more present than I have ever been because, quite honestly, I'm scared that any moments I've been taking for granted I may or may not get a chance to experience in the future. My definition of what makes a "great" day for me has changed significantly since my life before cancer. It has become more about the simple pleasures, like a good talk with my son, or a day out with my daughter.

Michelle completed treatment during the writing of this book, and I'm happy to share how she is doing. She told me, "I'm now through treatment and doing well, and I have a deep appreciation for how fragile life can be. I feel like I'm living now with my whole heart."

Sometimes it takes a life-changing event or a personal crisis to reach the end of ourselves and finally ask "What am I doing this all for?" Sometimes it takes someone in our lives to ask the question, "Are you truly living your values?" It is in those times that we have to be honest with ourselves and admit where we are in relation to the values that are meant to guide us to our real selves.

The Right Way to Build a Business

Thanks to the success my business once had, I was told that I should write a book about building a company the right way. I responded by saying, "No, that is not a book I can write."

I certainly built a company, but I didn't do it the *"right"* way, as I betrayed my values in the process. To the outside world, we were a massive success; a fast-growing business, with increasing revenues and award-winning performance. But, to me, building a business the "right way" means doing so while living your values, being the truest expression of yourself possible and being able to put as much into your personal relationships as you do your business.

I do not believe that building a company the "right way" is about forsaking all else for the good of the business. In fact, I believe that is utter failure, and while my first company received quite a bit of notoriety and I built my personal brand, I cannot write that it was a success due to the havoc it wreaked on my personal life and those I love dearly.

Living life by your values will impact what you do in business. I used to believe that I could be one person in my business role and then turn parts of that off to be my personal, non-business self. I thought I could invoke George Costanza and never let the worlds collide. That is a fallacy and is something that we as humans cannot do; not if we want to foster authentic relationships built on trust and founded on our core values.

An article in the *Harvard Business Review* once posed a poignant question, "Are values an essential ingredient of leadership?"[39]

It presented two schools of thought; leadership is often defined as a "simple matter of power and influence," meaning a leader is someone who "has followers." This, the authors argue, leads to the "Gandhi/Hitler problem."

Gandhi had a great many followers, but so did Hitler. If leadership is essentially a matter of power and influence, then both individuals must be deemed great by virtue of the fact that they both changed history and influenced the lives of millions. For anyone with a moral compass and respect for human dignity, however, that's an uncomfortable — actually, a repugnant assertion.

There is, of course, a different perspective; that leadership is all about values. That in order to understand leadership, you must consider where an individual is going, and why and how he or she is going there. An individual with tremendous influence who offers flawed diagnoses of communal challenges, "solutions" that fail to address real problems, and who operates with a fundamental disrespect for human dignity and interdependence is, actually, not a leader at all. In contrast, an individual whose influence extends no further than immediate family,

---

[39] Klau, M. (2010, May 27). Twenty-First-Century Leadership: It's All About Values. Harvard Business Review. Retrieved from https://hbr.org/2010/05/whose-values-the-gandhihitler.html

friends, and local community may well be a leader, if he or she is devoted to improving the human condition — at any scale.

Values are as critical to business as our financial acumen, management skills, or our ability to forge relationships. Some leaders integrate their values at a scale large enough to impact real, lasting change in the world.

As noted in *Forbes,*[40] Salesforce CEO Marc Benioff has personally overseen two equal pay assessments at his company. Both resulted in the company spending $3M to "eliminate statistically significant differences in pay". Salesforce also has a rule that at least 30% of meeting attendees must be women. The company was named as one of the 25 best companies for women in 2016. These positive steps towards gender equality uphold the idea that "the business of business is improving the state of the world" from Salesforce's Ohana Culture, which Benioff himself developed whilst on sabbatical in Hawaii.

I wonder what our corporations would look like if we all recognized the importance of truly living out our values? I wonder what changes we would see in the people we manage, those we work alongside and who we become if we truly made our values the guiding principles in our personal and professional lives? I know since renewing mine, I have reaped incredible rewards both personally and professionally, and I am more aware than ever of the need to cultivate and tend to them. I encourage you to do the same.

May we who are leading businesses, pursuing entrepreneurship and looking to make an impact do so with our values

---

[40] *Goldin, K. (2017, October 27). Why A Leader's Personal Values Are Essential To A Successful Brand. Forbes.*

directing our paths. May we be vigilant and first protect that which we value and guard against a slow decay of that which we hold dear. May we not only speak our values, may we live them, and use them as a guide to true success (in business and in all aspects of our lives.)

Reflection Questions:

1. What are your core values?

2. Are you currently living by your values?

3. If not, what needs to change to align your words and actions?

CHAPTER 11

Now and Then

"Love the life you live, live the life you love." —Bob Marley

At some time or another, all of us will come to an end. Like our lives, nothing lasts forever. Our businesses will end, our careers will run their course, and for those well-known in their industry, there will be someone who follows today who takes your place tomorrow. Nothing lasts forever, even though we may like to believe otherwise.

So, when it is all said and done, when the last page has finally turned, what traits will be assigned to you? What are the characteristics of the legacy that people will know you for? How do you want to be remembered? Or perhaps the better question is, how do you want to be known now?

I know those who are intent on making a name for themselves in the business world. In an age of personal branding, it is tempting to boost one's ego. In fact, it's one of the things that once drove me. But, when we peel back all of the layers of accomplishment, all of the professional achievements and vanity, to truly reveal our core, what is left for people to know and remember us by? Beyond the superficial accolades, what are we leaving behind?

For some, the first step in answering these questions is getting to the core of who we truly are, tapping into the nature that was created in us and allowing our true selves to be known. That's often easier said than done.

For too many years I, both unconsciously and consciously, tried to keep my true self hidden, projecting a persona in its place. By nature, I am a very sensitive person. I cry easily, and my emotions can be stirred by simple things. Additionally, I am not motivated by money or material things. Wealth has never impressed me. I feel more comfortable in a pair of jeans and a hoodie then I do in a fancy pair of shoes and a suit. When I look at myself, I believe I am a pretty simple guy with pretty simple taste and not all that hard to please.

However, the more I bought into my ego, the more that changed. My emotions were shut off. My younger brother once asked, "Dude, are you ok? You do not seem like yourself," to which I responded, "I am numb, I really do not feel anything much anymore."

In addition to building a wall around my emotions, I began to put value in material things. I started buying suits and cufflinks and wore them at industry events and client meetings. I took great pride (false pride) when I would get a compliment on one of my watches. I would insist on staying in the nicest hotels and get upset when I did not get an upgrade, like those things really speak to my value anyway.

While there is nothing fundamentally wrong with any of those things, they were wrong for me, as that is not who I am.

When I look at getting back to and honoring my true self, I see the changes. I have not worn a suit in two years, I do not care about my upgrades, my airline status, my cufflinks or my watches. I am back in touch with my emotions and cry and laugh more easily than ever before. This shift is right, for this is part of me and my true self. I like these things about myself and no longer am trying to hide them.

When you can get to the core of who you are and furthermore embrace your true self, you will be at your best in all aspects of life and this is one of the things I found will shine through in your leadership and how you build an organization.

In the movie *Dead Poets Society*[41], new teacher John Keating, played by Robin Williams, teaches at the prestigious and rather stuffy, all boys Welton Academy. On the first day of class, the newly appointed Keating enters the classroom from his office door whistling blissfully as he walks by his teenage students into the hallway. Noticing they are reluctant to follow, he gleefully summons them to join him. As they pour out from the classroom and into the hallway, they find themselves standing in front of the history of the school's sports program enshrined behind the glass of an expansive trophy case. Within the case are pictures of former Welton students from previous years going back decades.

Keating invites one of his students to read the first verse of the poem *To The Virgins, To Make Much of Time* by Robert Herrick, which reads, "Gather ye rosebuds while ye may, Old Time is still a-flying; And this same flower that smiles today Tomorrow will be dying." At Keating's urging, the boys press in and around the trophy case as he tells them that those boys in the picture are much like them, but are now "fertilizing daffodils."

---

[41] Weir, P. (Director). (1989). Dead Poets Society [Motion picture]. USA: Buena Vista Pictures Distribution.

All of us, will one day be just like the boys in the photo. We too will be gone and will have left something behind – a legacy that depends on what we do now.

I know, for me, that I do not want my children or close of relationships remembering me as a man who worked tirelessly, who was a business builder, or merely a maker of companies. I want them to remember me as a loyal friend, and a loving father and husband. I want to be known as a man who put family first, and who was selfless. This is the legacy I want to leave. It's one that is long-lasting, but I realized that the work to leave this kind of legacy has to start now.

What About Now?

There is a bumper sticker I have seen from time-to-time in Colorado Springs that reads, "All You Have is Now." It's so simple, but so profoundly true.

None of us is guaranteed tomorrow. There is no promise that you will walk into your job tomorrow and still have it, as I experienced. There is no guarantee that your biggest client won't walk out the door to your competitor, and there is no guarantee that you will wake up tomorrow at all. All we can be guaranteed of is the here and now.

Yet, so many of us waste the "now" and exchange it for something that may never come; future promotion; acquisition; riches; or fame.

Given that all we have is now, today, what are we doing to make our lives extraordinary? Most importantly, how are we defining that?

In that same *Dead Poets Society* scene, Keating goes onto to introduce the curious boys to the Latin phrase "carpe diem," which those of us familiar with the film knows translates to "seize the day." Keating takes on the voice of those in the photographs who can no longer speak themselves. He whispers the message, "carpe diem." Keating encourages his young students to "seize the day," and to make their lives extraordinary.

This message is one that we should *all* take to heart.

If we haven't started the process by now, we must explore what will make our lives truly *extraordinary*, what will allow us to imbibe in the present, and to experience the thrill that awaits us in our lives and in our relationships.

Is it *really* the number of hours we work? Waking up at the "hustlers hour" so we can make it just a bit further than our competition? Is living an extraordinary life translated only to working harder, sacrificing health and family for the sake of some elusive dream?

I don't believe so, as I have lived both sides and can assure you the riches lie in relationships and living for the present moment (even the simplest ones).

So, like Keating asked of his students, ask yourself the following question: What is truly "extraordinary?" We are building our legacies by our actions today. How do people know you, and what are you showing them with each action you take?

Many of us have tried to achieve someone else's definition of "extraordinary" by building something of worth, by accumulating wealth, by racking up business achievements and being assigned lofty titles. We have defined the "extraordinary" by things that have little eternal value or purpose, and in so doing have missed the point entirely. We have also missed the beauty of deeply knowing those around us and being known in return.

Our lives and our dreams should not be defined or confined to the companies we start and grow. They should not be measured by the heights of our career, and they should not be calculated by the growth of our material possessions or bank accounts.

Our dreams should be routed in the reality of who we were made to be and what gifts and talents our maker has bestowed upon us. They should be measured by the depths of our relationships, our ability to love, to laugh, and to experience joy with those we hold most dear, those we value, and those who have equal affinity for us.

The wonderful thing is that life presents us with a daily opportunity to right the course. We can fulfill our purpose, find our true selves and enjoy all the joy and marrow that life provides as we lead, as we progress in our careers, as we build businesses and pursue our entrepreneurial adventures. The key is not to confuse the point of it all. It is not an "either/or" scenario. A fulfilled life can foster business success within it. We don't need to trade fulfillment for achievement.

Embrace the "And"

Rather than live by an "either/or" mantra, embrace the idea of "and."

You can succeed, even wildly, in business *and* you can still live a fruitful, blessed and fulfilling life with life-giving relationships, joy, health and happiness. However, you have to subscribe to a different path than the common refrain I often hear of "burning the candle at both ends" in order to make it happen.

It may take you time to find that thing, that note, or your passion. It will likely take even more time to discover your *true self.* However, I urge you to start down that road now as this is the only time you truly have to do it.

As the saying goes, the best time to plant a tree was 20 years ago. The second-best time is now.

I hope this book has given you the encouragement to stop chasing a dream that has been fabricated and marketed well, without the ugly truth of its impact on our lives. I hope that your own pursuit of happiness is not derailed by the idea that to live the American Dream is to burn out, neglect relationships and always be connected to an unforgiving master.

The truth is, you deserve more, and there is a better way. May you do the work to find it and may you begin to reject all that is UnAmerican and chase the dream that will bring true happiness and fulfillment.

Reflection Questions:

1. What legacy do you want to leave behind?

2. What steps can you take to make your life extraordinary - beyond the superficial labels of success we are conditioned to rely on?

3. What are you doing today to define what your legacy will be tomorrow?

CHAPTER 12

Some Parting Words

"It's never too late to mend your ways." —*American Proverb*

Throughout the pages of this book, I have attempted to tell my story and at the same time use it as a means of encouragement. I do believe that we often do our fellow man and ourselves a disservice if we do not share what we have learned from our failings. In many respects that is what this book is about.

I hope that through the pages of this book, you have felt challenged in some way to look at your personal and professional life differently. If you have reassessed and, with the honest input of others, believe you have a good thing going and have struck a healthy balance, then good on you! I hope you will share how you got there with others at every opportunity.

If, however, you have read through the pages of this book and related to some of my journey, we both know you can do better. I encourage you to begin making the changes today. Don't wait to see how things are going to pan out. Deep down, you already know the answer. Let my own rock bottom be a warning. Things will not magically change, you simply have to put forth the effort and make some fundamental shifts in your life if you want to see different results.

For some, this may mean changing jobs, downsizing, and even scaling back on expenses. If this is what it will take for you to be healthy, get the most from your relationships and be the best version of you in both your personal and professional life, then this is what should be done.

My last bit of advice was told to me early in my journey by a good friend, who said, "Be patient and be gentle with yourself."

My friend knew that I, like most with Type A personalities, are neither patient nor gentle in critique of ourselves. The truth is, this is exactly what is needed throughout this process. It will take time for you to make the changes needed and to adapt to your new self, new way of working, and your realignment of values and priorities. At times, you will fail; the beauty of it, however, is that failure, endurance, pain and relief are all part of the process, and with the right mindset, you can learn from every step you take.

May we who pursue a new path be bold, be courageous, and choose not to go it alone. May we all find the true meaning of the American Dream!

My TEDx Speech

⬤━⬤━⬤━⬤

In November of 2018 I was invited to deliver my first TEDx speech "Setting Work-Life Boundaries" at the TEDxCentennialParkWomen event. The speech was delivered to approximately 450 women and is the essence of the book. Below is the text of my speech.

Here's one of the easiest polls you'll ever take. Raise your hand if you've heard of work-life balance?

Now, raise your hand if you've heard of work-life blend. It's not as popular as work-life balance. But, it's this idea that, "I'm not really going to give all of myself to work life or personal life. Instead, I'm going to mesh it all together." While both of these concepts are not altogether foreign, today I would like to discuss a third view called work-life boundaries.

If I am in your shoes, I am sitting there asking myself, what is a man going to tell 400 women about work-life balance, blend or boundaries? I appreciate that and perhaps if I were in your shoes would ask the same question.

To answer that, I believe it is first vitally important to address two perspectives in our culture that have been widely adopted as truth that I believe are just flat wrong.

The first perspective is that of a career woman. There is an expectation that when work is over, it is the woman who needs to be the one primarily responsible for taking care of things at home, making sure the kids do their homework, get shuttled to practice, get fed, are in bed on time, etc.

For men, there is also an idea that has been widely accepted that is equally wrong. It is expected and accepted that we are not as connected at home, not as emotive, that somehow, we are more devoted to our work, working longer hours and draining ourselves to the point where we have nothing left and due to this there is an expectation that we don't contribute equally to the well-being of our homes.

So, let me first state that I believe both of these widely-accepted role descriptions should be rejected and that this is not me, a man, telling you women to adopt my boundaries, but it is me encouraging you to take a look at living a life that is incorporates boundaries and in so doing create more opportunities for you to show up.

I hate to say it, but much of my career could be described as living a life way off-balance. I was one that accepted the warped perception of what my role as dad and husband should be and I was certainly devoid of any semblance of boundaries and as a result was not doing my equal share in our home.

In fact, you could say I was committed to this unbalanced way of life, so much so, that in 2014 I wrote this post on LinkedIn:

In this post I stated, "I am completely unbalanced and I am ok with that!"

So, let me go back. In early 2002, I landed a job with a global, brand name software company. I quickly found success and was recognized by the company for my contributions. Over the course of the next several years, my ascent up the corporate ladder led to longer hours and continuous travel which meant I was missing games, concerts, and a good majority of our dinners. However, I convinced myself it was worth it as I was doing it for my family. Truth is they did not care about my title, my promotions, my raises or the accolades I received, they wanted me home, to be present and to be a dad and a husband who was involved and available.

Towards the end of my run with the software company, I had an overnight trip to Austin, TX. We lived in Dallas at the time so to me it was a short trip, one night and less than 45 minutes of flight time. I got settled into my hotel and called home. My youngest Luke, who was three at the time answered and quickly asked, "Daddy, are you on an airplane?" With a laugh I told him, "No buddy, I am in a hotel." With that answer he responded, "You're always in a hotel!" and he hung up.

I was crushed and feebly said hello in the hopes that he had not hung up, but I knew he did. I also knew that he, like the rest of my family, were fed up and he was right, I was always in hotels.

My wife, Susanne, called back and she apologized, however, she was not the one who needed to apologize, I was. It was that night I realized things had to change and told Susanne, "I can't continue to do this" and she quickly agreed.

Shortly thereafter I left the software company and co-founded my first business. It was a big risk and I was scared. I had never done business ownership before and did not know what the future would hold, but I did know that it would keep me home and allow me to be more involved in the lives of those I loved so dearly. My family was also on board. We knew financially this would be a big step backward, but having more time as a family was well worth it.

The first few years of the business went as any small business does, full of ups and downs but then things started to take off. Before long, our business grew, we began getting larger clients, we began adding employees, my travel was increasing, our growth was continual. Not only was the business thriving, but I was establishing a personal brand in my industry, I was being asked to speak, write, offer my opinions in industry publications, I signed a contract to write my first book. I was repeating the very cycle I vowed to break, but this time was worse.

If I am honest, in looking back, what drove me more than anything was ego. I loved the accolades, I loved being known in our space, it fed my ego to get the next brand name client, I loved seeing my name on a book and I was more than ok with being completely unbalanced as after all, I was "successful".

The truth is that the more success I had and the more the business grew, the less fulfilled and more narcissistic I became. But why? If I was so successful and achieving so much, how had I become so miserable? It is because the thing that was missing was meaningful relationship . . . which is fundamentally what we are humans are wired for!

I was moving so fast and so consumed with my drive to succeed, that I put my relationships on the back burner and focused on what I thought was best, what I thought would feed me and be life giving. But it wasn't. In late 2015, I came to a crossroads. I could continue to focus on my career, invest in the façade of business success and in the process lose my marriage and family or I could focus and invest in my marriage and relationship with my children which are the things that bring true joy.

While it took me twice around to learn (I have been known to be a slow learner), I knew that this time had to change and that change had to have permanence.

My establishment of work-life boundaries did not begin immediately, it was and continues to be a journey. It began with making some conscious choices. The first of which was the business.

After wrestling with the decision for 10 months, at the end of 2016 I told my business partners I was leaving the agency I helped start 11 years prior. I had no plan B, no back-up plan, no big buyout and no job waiting. As one friend called it, I simply pulled the ripcord. As big of a risk as this was for my wife and I, I felt so assured that this was the right choice to make.

The next thing I needed to do was to slow down. The frenetic pace I had been keeping and the speed at which I had been moving was preventing me from hearing those around me who loved me and could see things that I simply could not see.

It was not until I decided to slow down that I could then take a few steps back and begin to determine what the next chapter would look like and what kind of life my wife and I wanted together and with our children. This time it was not me making the decision in isolation, it was a series of discussions, me taking the time to listen and view this from a different perspective. It was me, with the help of others, seeking to do this holistically as after all I was far from the only person impacted by my choices.

Additionally, I had to apologize and admit that the me-first, career-first approach that I had been living was wrong. As part of that process, I went back to LinkedIn and published this post – "I Was Wrong".

In this post, I quote Brené Brown who states the following, "If we want to live a wholehearted life, we have to become intentional about cultivating sleep and play, and about letting go of exhaustion as a status symbol and productivity as self-worth."

I was far from living a wholehearted life, was not cultivating the things that brought me the most joy, and I did tie my productivity and accolades to self-worth and in the process was oblivious to the slow erosion of my closest relationships.

Two years have passed since I began my boundary-guided journey and I am glad to let you know that things are incredibly different.

My wife and I decided that I should begin another company, but this time Susanne is my only business partner. Secondly, we jointly decided that we would be a purpose-driven company. We demonstrate this by giving 5% of our profits to a nonprofit that serves single moms and widows in Uganda. Secondly, my wife Susanne is now my business partner.

We have documented the boundaries that we strive to live by and we discuss them regularly to ensure we are living within them.

While these boundaries are working for us, you will have to determine what your boundaries look like as these boundaries would have been far different when our children were younger and they will be different for you whether you are married, single, have kids or no kids. The key is to define them and do them in community with your closest of relationships.

One of your boundaries may be that at least one time per week, you are going to take time out to do something just for you. It may be a massage, going to a movie alone, taking a walk with no phone or going on a date with your significant other. Your boundaries do not have to be grand, they just need to be established. You have to determine what is best for you.

The beauty of living within boundaries are the clear lines that are drawn.

When I am working, I am working. This is my boundary. I am not giving myself to multiple things, I am focused, mindful and deliberate about the work I am doing during the time I am living within my work boundary.

At the same time, when I am focused on my relationships, my hobbies and the things outside of work that bring me joy, I am wholly there and completely vested without any work distractions.

The outcome has been a wealth of creativity, a renewed sense of exploration both personally and professionally. My relationships are stronger, my work product is better, my thinking is clearer, my emotional, mental, physical and spiritual health are better than they have ever been and the list goes on.

I do not know what your boundaries will look like, I do not know your individual stories, but you now know a little of mine and I implore you to go home tonight and just begin writing some of the boundaries you believe you need to establish and then discuss them with a loved one.

I can tell you that my boundaries have saved me, they help keep me centered and have now become a way of life that I continually strive to live by. It is noticeable and this was no more apparent than when my daughter Lauren, as she was preparing to leave for college told me, "Dad, I really love the guy you are now . . . I just wished he had not taken so long to show up."

Thank you!

Corporate Profiles

If you are reading this section of the book, you have either jumped ahead or finished the book, and if the latter is true, I hope it was an encouragement for you. As I spent well over the last year writing, I at times found suspicious looks when I shared the concept of the book. The phrase that inevitably followed was, "I could never do some of these things because of . . ." I would also often hear, "Well, you can do the things you talk about because you work for yourself."

While I do appreciate those sentiments and where they come from, I have come to believe that ultimately, they are rooted in fear. While many of us know changes need to be made, our fear of that change gets to a point where we erect monuments to the excuses as to why we cannot.

One of the joys I did experience when writing this book was more hopeful than what I just described. I met scores of people who, upon hearing my journey, began sharing their own, or sending me links to articles of others who had made similar adjustments. I was connected with people who resonated with my story and wanted to hear more of it. It was through these conversations that I realized I had to share a few profiles of the amazing and brave women and men that I met throughout this journey.

I tell their stories here to first give them a round of applause on finding their true joy while, and at the same time, protecting what is important. I also include them as evidence that you too can make changes, you too can be successful no matter if you own your company, work for another, are a man or woman, or any other excuse.

You simply have to want it and have the courage to pursue it.

1. *"Guarding Her American Dream"*

Claire Potter - Director of Institutional Sales Support

I had the pleasure of meeting Claire in Atlanta after I gave my TEDx talk. She told me that the talk resonated deeply with her and was something she and her husband had recently been discussing, especially since the arrival of their first child five months earlier.

Claire works for one of the largest investment management companies in the country and has found success moving through the corporate ranks. Her story was inspirational to me and she was kind enough to grant me an interview in which she gave her perspective on her values and how she, together with her husband, are guarding their American Dream.

CH: There are many demands placed on individuals when working for a large company. What were the demands placed on you in your role? How did those impact you when you had your first child?

CP: In sales, frequent travel plays a large part of the role. In my former role, I was covering client relationships in the Northeast out of Atlanta. My team had a reorganization while I was out on maternity, and I came back into this role. As you can imagine, doing so after having my first child meant there were many more logistics to figure out, and the role required longer trips and time away.

My husband also travels frequently, so after about eight months of juggling our "new normal" with both of us on the road as much as we were, we knew something had to change in order for us to manage it all successfully and with minimal stress.

CH: *What values were you looking to protect by changing your job role?*

CP: I wanted to protect both my personal and professional goals. Personally, I place a very high value on being present and involved with my family. Knowing that time is precious, I don't want to look back on these years with regret that I wasn't making my family a priority.

As for my professional goals, I desire to be instrumental in meaningful work which allows me to feel fulfilled. I also get a lot of joy by putting my education, certifications and industry knowledge to work. In seeking this fulfillment, I felt I was ready for a challenge in a different way by taking on people management to continue to build my skill set. This was a large component I wove into the new role that I was planning to take to my management.

CH: *What steps did you take with your company to protect those values?*

CP: When I had made my mind up that something had to give, I thought of ways where I could still add value to my team and meet my need for professional fulfillment, but in a different capacity that didn't require the extensive travel.

I spent time crafting a job description for a new role that served as a solution for me both personally and professionally, as well as the business. This solutions-oriented approach was very well-received by management throughout my conversations with them as I wasn't just bringing them a problem, but instead had sought out a need for the firm that aligned both my strengths and prior experience in the industry. This became the role I'm in now.

CH: You took a big risk that may not have played out as you had hoped. What were you prepared to do if your company was not receptive to your request to redefine your corporate role?

CP: Knowing that a new headcount is very difficult to come by since we just had a large reorganization on my team, I had started speaking with various recruiters and attending networking events in the event that the firm wasn't able to accommodate my request. In that time, I had become very active on LinkedIn and was looking at various other roles at other firms.

Thankfully they were very receptive and I was able to assume the new role. Today I feel I am making a difference at the company while not sacrificing time with my family and my closest relationships.

CH: How has your life changed since you have defined your new role and defined what you are willing to do, and not do?

CP: The new role has created more normalcy and consistency at home so that at least one parent is there to have that time with our daughter each day. There is still a travel component to this new role, but it's much more predictable and less frequent so that my husband can ensure he's at home with our daughter when I have to travel. The stress level in the house has certainly gone down now that we don't have to juggle the competing meetings, trips and priorities!

One component that I also negotiated when I was in talks about the new role is working from home one day a week, which is not typically standard in my company. Although that seems marginal, as a working mother, that one day a week where you don't have to get yourself ready, get your child ready, drop your child off and then get yourself into the office is so valuable. That one day at home also allows me to cut out the commute, begin working earlier, and be completely focused with little distraction.

CH: What advice would you give to other women (or men) who find themselves in a similar position?

CP: It's daunting to realize that something has to change in order to make all aspects of your life and the values you hold dear function, especially after becoming a parent and trying to settle in to your "new normal." The process seems to be filled with guilt that you're no longer "great" at any one thing, like you were before this life-changing event.

I do wonder if I will ever have that true feeling of work-life balance, but do think that it is possible to figure out what it will take to fulfill your personal and professional goals and protect those values simultaneously.

I believe it's important to keep in mind that the reputation you have at your present company will allow conversations like the one I had with management at my company to have a higher likelihood of being well-received. In all likelihood, they will be receptive to try to retain strong female talent coming up within the organization.

If you go into those conversations prepared and take a solutions-oriented approach rather than just posing a problem, it takes the heavy lifting off management and also shows commitment to the organization and initiative to identify an existing need within the company.

2. *"Defining a Life from the Inside-Out"*

Brian Carroll - Founder and CEO of markempa

I have had the pleasure of knowing Brian Carroll for a number of years. When we first met, Brian had recently sold his first business and was working for the firm who had made the purchase. From a corporate perspective, he had found success. Our second, much more meaningful interaction came as Brian was in the middle of determining what his next chapter would look like.

Brian had been back working on his own for a year now and was kind enough to grant me an interview to talk about his version of the American Dream.

CH: What is your definition of the American Dream?

BC: For me, the American Dream is about living my purpose on my terms and values rather than what others expect of me. It's about living life without compromising my non-negotiables (like self-care, health, exercise, family, vacation, the pursuit of interests, spiritual, values) and feeling free to choose how to live on my terms.

CH: What motivates you in the professional position in which you now hold?

BC: In the big picture, I want to feel that what I'm doing is making a difference and having an impact, while ideally being a force for good.

I work closely with those in the marketing profession and care about my clients. I want to help those who also feel like me know that what we're doing is making a difference inside organizations. This goes beyond just making money.

CH: You have started your second company. How has entrepreneurship impacted your view of the American Dream?

BC: I often feel people define the American Dream as getting more things like wealth, material possessions, fame, prestige, security, and more. I'm not saying those are bad things. However, those things are more likely to happen when you put someone else's needs ahead of your own by serving others, adding value, and making a difference. Yes, greed can enter in. However, that's a fact in any work we undertake. At its core, entrepreneurship is about serving others' unmet (and sometimes unarticulated) needs. When we learn to serve others and care, we're curious, we apply empathy to see from their perspective, and we help. It changes us. I haven't found a business that's been successful where customers didn't benefit.

CH: If you could do it all over and start again, what would you do differently?

BC: When I first started as an entrepreneur, I was 23 years old. I would say that I lived outside-in rather than inside-out.

Here's what I mean:

I would set a goal for myself focused on external things, whether that be my income, getting things like a nice house in a nice neighborhood, how many children I wanted, finding a beautiful wife, getting well-known in my industry, or building an Inc. 500 company.

In sum, I wanted to be *externally* successful so that others could see these things, but deep down I was trying to change how I felt inside by curating how I looked outside. To put it another way, I didn't want to be successful; I wanted to look the part of what I thought a successful entrepreneur looks like on the outside. I look back, and though I achieved a lot, I often felt like an impostor, because I was living life to try to fit someone else's definition of success.

Now, I live inside out. My highest focus is to be authentic and bring my whole self to life. I don't feel a conflict between my work and home life because of who I am as a person. My worth is no longer determined by my work or status. I'm finding that I'm happier and more content today because I'm operating out of my natural place of being. I started my new company being clear on my non-negotiables, my values, relationship priorities, and why I'm doing what I'm doing and beyond making money.

CH: What three things would you tell an entrepreneur or someone moving up the corporate ladder that you wish you had known?

BC: I would first say to get clear on how you define success and what you want, because if you don't, the world and others around you will define it for you.

Secondly, I would encourage you to be clear on the tradeoffs you're making as you pursue your goals and growth. This may seem obvious, but looking back, I sacrificed too much time with my kids and wife. This isn't something I would repeat.

Lastly, I would tell you to set aside time for self-examination and reflection. Someone could work for 30 years and repeat the same mistakes 30 times. Wisdom doesn't come from how long we live or work. It comes from being aware and willing to see things differently.

3: "Life is Short"

Elle Woulfe - VP of Marketing; PathFactory

I have had the pleasure to know Elle Woulfe for a number of years and have had the good fortune to collaborate with her on a few projects during that time. Elle is an accomplished executive who has exemplified balancing her career while prioritizing her family.

CH: You have mentioned that early on in your career you determined that when the time came for you to have a family, you would make them the top priority. Was there a certain experience that helped shape that?

EW: I have been pretty ruthless in my pursuit of balance and always will be.

One of my very first jobs out of college was at a research and consulting firm where many of the consultants travelled a ton and worked crazy hours. I would hear them talking all the time about how they hadn't seen their families in days or how they missed their kids' games. They thought it was a badge of honor, but I just thought it was sad. I never wanted to be the kind of person whose self-worth was measured in hours away from my family.

CH: How has having a family shaped your thinking and choices on your career?

EW: I was 36 when I had my first child and I think that was also formative for me. I was very aware that I was a little older and I just appreciated every minute with my daughter so very much.

I have made very conscious choices to protect the balance I have created in my life. Everyone thought I had lost my mind when I left my former job at Lattice Engines to join a startup like Look-BookHQ (now PathFactory). Lattice was well-funded, further along in its lifecycle, and I had a really good gig. But, each day I commuted into the city and even though it was flexible, it was a grind.

A really big part of why I joined this scrappy, early-stage start-up was because I would be able to work from home. Being able to drop my kids off at school and pick them up and take them to activities was worth any pay cut.

I still have to travel a bit but it's manageable, and I work for Canadians who have amazing family values and are incredibly respectful of the choices I make to protect my own values. I keep all my trips as short as possible and I say no to a lot.

CH: What have been some of the biggest benefits you have seen from putting your focus on your personal life instead of your career?

EW: First and foremost, I have gotten to be so present in the lives of my kids while they are little and it's something I would never trade for anything. And I honestly don't think I gave up much, maybe a bigger job or a little more money but certainly not happiness. This extends to other parts of my life. I play on a tennis team and I train for half-marathons, much of which occurs during business hours.

I don't feel the least bit guilty about it about it because I work my butt off and I deliver a ton of value to the business. So, I do the things that are important to me and bring me joy. That's how they get the best from me.

CH: What would you tell other people who are struggling with their current job or weighing a change in career?

EW: For me, there is no other way. I recently had a very cool opportunity come my way. It would have been a great boost to my career. It would have been super high-profile and I was so flattered to even be considered. But I knew right away that it wasn't an option as it was going to require more than I can give right now.

I could literally see the lack of balance the role would require when I was talking to the CEO. I would have to give up too much and I knew I would lose in the long run.

Life is short. I want to know I was there for it.

4: "The Freedom to Create What's Meaningful"

Samantha Stone - Founder of the Marketing Advisory Network

I first met Samantha a number of years ago when she and I both were participants in a panel at a marketing event in Boston. She was in the early stages of her company and she had boundless energy and optimism that was refreshing. Over the course of the last few years, she has become a trusted colleague.

CH: Starting a business is not for the faint of heart. What motivated you to leave corporate America and start your own business?

SS: Six years ago I was in a job I liked, but didn't love. I started looking for a new position and went on several interviews. I was talking to a few great companies where my skills would drive a measurable impact. Nothing excited me. I picked up a couple of consulting projects to tide me over while I searched for the right job and used this time to reflect on what I wanted to be doing.

The more successful I had become, the further away I travelled from the work I loved. I was spending so much time in board meetings, executive sessions and juggling internal politics that it had stopped being joyful. At the same time, my boys were getting older and I was feeling distance growing between us, which was painful.

Ultimately, I craved more control of where and what I worked on. I didn't know it at first, but those consulting projects were a beacon. I realized I could provide huge value and impact to an organization without being an employee – something I had not seriously considered prior.

Seven years later I can honestly say I don't regret a single day running my own business. It's not always easy, but it has always felt right.

CH: How has entrepreneurship impacted your view of the American Dream?

SS: While I was born in the United States, and have always called it home, I spent much of my childhood outside the country. As such, the American Dream has always been a bit of a mix for me. I always viewed it as both financial and political freedom – the ultimate in stability and elimination of uncertainty.

Over the years, I've come to believe that the American Dream is about freedom, but not the same kind I used to imagine. It's about freedom to create something meaningful, which may or may not come with financial stability, but it almost always includes a measure of uncertainty.

CH: *If you could do it all over and start again, what would you do differently?*

SS: If I had it all to do again, I'd still work in corporate life. I'd still build years of experience and an amazing network of talented colleagues that would become the foundation for The Marketing Advisory Network. But, I would like to believe I would have learned three important lessons sooner.

First, I would learn to trust the people around me faster. It's not about working the hardest, it's about exceeding expectations. I eventually got good at saying "yes, but" explaining what had to come off my plate (and given to someone else) to give me time on a new project, but it took too long to get there.

Second, I'd work much harder at enjoying the journey. I'd learn sooner about different communication and work styles and adapt to different approaches with more ease and less discomfort.

Third, and this is perhaps the most important lesson of all, I'd make sure there was time for me in all of the running-around that comes with being a parent and a professionally ambitious woman. My work and my kids were so all-consuming I forgot to nurture myself; my friendships, my hobbies, even just the pleasure of doing nothing, was lost. If I could go back in time, I'd make sure that sacrifice was not made nearly as often.

CH: *How do you define work-life balance?*

SS: Work-life balance has never been about the amount of time I spend on one thing vs. another. It's about the amount of fulfilment I can achieve in any moment of time.

Do I feel guilty when I'm missing a conference call to enjoy dinner with my family?

Do I wake up in a cold sweat, frustrated about a professional project?

Am I annoyed at having to read another bedtime story?

For most of my career I was in a constant state of annoyed frustration because I was pulled in too many directions.

But no more. For me, work-life balance has become about giving my whole self to whatever task is at hand including working out, laughing with friends, cuddling with my kids or presenting to a room full of colleagues, all without feeling guilty or distracted.

CH: *What is your core focus now as an entrepreneur? (Family, job, clients, etc?)*

SS: When I launched my company I wasn't sure how long I'd be operating it, but I always ran the company as if it was a long-term decision. I've had the good fortune to flex work and family in all the best ways as a result.

For example, when my son had a serious illness I didn't have any anxiety about skipping meetings to take him to neurologists. Conversely, when a client was acquired, I didn't hesitate to cancel plans with friends to help them write their communications strategy.

Unlike the past, these decisions felt natural because I was now happy with both my work and my private life and I knew when I felt good about saying yes, and when a no was needed. I had control to make decisions that were good for me and my family.

I expected this personal and professional balance; or, at least, it's what I hoped would happen. However, an extra bonus has developed (which was unexpected); personal growth. The way we work is changing dramatically and as a small business owner it would be tempting to stick with what I know best. However, with some planning I've made time to explore new areas of interest that have made me a more creative person, and a better strategist.

5: *"Moving from Success to Significance"*

Glen Jackson - Co-Founder of Jackson Spaulding

I had the privilege of meeting Glen Jackson at a reception his company was hosting, where we spoke about business and life. He shared some of his story and the values that he holds and instills in Jackson Spalding, his award-winning marketing communications agency.

CH: *As a son of a World War II veteran, what does the term "the UnAmerican Dream" mean for you?*

GJ: This is a probing and somewhat shocking statement to absorb. My first reaction to the phrase "the UnAmerican dream" is one, I have to admit as the son of a D-Day tank driver, of serious pause. It strikes me as the antithesis of what my dad believed in while fighting valiantly on the beaches of Normandy, France on June 6th, 1944. Thinking about it more, it makes me consider what this phrase really means at its deepest core and how it differs from the phrase "the American Dream."

Is the American Dream really alive and realistic now? (I hope and believe it is quite attainable, by the way.) How do we define such a phrase today? What does it look like and what parts of such a definition are *still* healthy and vibrant and *now* perhaps unhealthy and challenging?

So, all in all, the "UnAmerican Dream" phrase is a thought-provoking one.

CH: *Your business, Jackson Spalding, is in its 24th year and you have had great business success. What have you learned over the years about finding success in your personal and professional life?*

GJ: Our business has certainly grown over the years, and we have been fortunate as we have scaled our business with entrepreneurial vigor and an entrepreneurial mindset. The word "success" is an interesting term. What does it truly mean in today's frenetic world?

As one gets older, you realize the importance of working smarter not harder. You pace yourself better this way, preserve precious energy for the bursts that are needed and, in turn, you become even more valued because it is where you are most valuable. The key here is to develop goals each year that zoom in on your biggest strengths; focusing on what you do best and delegating the rest, as the sage Bob Buford talks about in his timeless book, *Halftime.*

Being narrow and deep here and creating relational depth with the people who matter most to you personally and professionally, which is where life has its deepest meaning.

To add to this, I would say that that becoming and remaining significant is more important than becoming and remaining successful in the long run. It might mean less money, less power, or less spotlight, per se, but it means more influence and genuine impact and satisfaction. You can change lives this way, and that is a pretty good return on investment.

CH: Today's business leaders and entrepreneurs are being told by many that in order to succeed, they need to "hustle" or be prepared to work 24/7 to succeed. What do you say to that?

GJ: Working 24/7 takes a toll on you, your family, and your friends. It is not a good formula to embrace or champion from my vantage point. It eventually catches up with you. Working hard is important – staying humble and hungry is how I describe it - but this does not mean working yourself to death. Your family does not become the benefactor here.

All in all, know now how to pace yourself and know when to take a much-needed respite. Find a good rhythm to your work day. To use a musical analogy, embrace a symphonic approach to your day (more Beethoven than Bad Company!) and avoid getting sucked into the bang-bang pressure of the world.

As much as you can, strive to work smarter, not harder. This requires discipline, but it can be done with the right mindset and unswerving commitment. You will benefit, and the people you love will as well. Strength for the journey here.

CH: If you could go back to the beginning of your entrepreneurial endeavor, what would you tell yourself?

GJ: I think I would tell myself to relax more and trust God even more; to not worry as much as I did when I was 32 and getting the business rolling with an amazing group of people. We have not tried to be a disruptor in our field, but instead enhancers and innovators. I would not change this mindset because it has been helpful to us.

On the mindset front, I would try to have more fun in the early years when we were just striving to survive. I took it too seriously, worked all the time and lost touch with my wife in the process, which was a terrible thing. I would like to go back and fix that, of course. It is not something I am particularly proud of as a man. My wife and I celebrate 34 years of marriage this year. I'm really blessed here.

CH: In speaking with an employee who works at Jackson Spalding, she commented to me that there is a "human first" culture. Can you provide more insight on that and what you do to instill that kind of culture into the organization?

GJ: Culture is a big, important word in business. I heard a CEO speak yesterday – he leads a large and immensely respected company in Atlanta – and he said culture is their most strategic asset. I agree with that. The best cultures have, at the core, a real focus on people and pouring into these folks and creating the best learning environment possible. They create a place where the ideas are free-flowing, and there are no walls around folks. Team members are treated as adults, with the utmost respect, and are part of the cultural mix and fabric. They contribute big time here.

The leader is not the culture, everyone is. Culture thrives when the word is not used all the time but is lived out and exemplified effortlessly, every day, as folks actualize their potential and have large and small bonding traditions that create a true esprit des corps with everyone. Their light shines brightly externally and the cultural DNA permeates internally.

Made in the USA
Columbia, SC
27 July 2019